Sounds of Hope

Sounds of Hope

A Musical Metaphor to Build a Symphony of Hope

Robert N. Janacek

WIPF & STOCK · Eugene, Oregon

SOUNDS OF HOPE
A Musical Metaphor to Build a Symphony of Hope

Wipf and Stock
An imprint of Wipf and Stock Publishers
199 W. 8th Ave., Suite 3
Eugene, OR 97401

www.wipfandstock.com

ISBN 13: 978-1-61097-657-2
Manufactured in the U.S.A.

Contents

*To my loving wife, Pat, who brings harmony to my life
and to those of countless others.*

Preface

HOPE IS AT THE heart of living a meaningful life. Hope is essential in facing such realities as sickness, death, injury, loss, wars, poverty, unemployment, cruelty, etc. So many of the huge questions that confront us as to the worth, fullness, and meaningfulness of life are answered only in the context of hope.

Emily Dickinson affirms the fundamental nature of hope in her poem on "Hope." "Hope is the thing with feathers / That perches in the soul, / And sings the tune—without the words, / And never stops at all . . ."

This adventure in reading about hope is a profound listening to music from various intellectual disciplines (philosophy, theology, psychology, and cosmology) that synthesize into a symphony of well-grounded hope in all aspects of life. We will gain evidence to support our faith in hope in spite of all the challenges that could discourage or despair us. May your understanding of hope in its various intellectual perspectives be enriched.

May your existential belief and trust in hope for your life be deepened and broadened. May your trust in hope in the face of the worst that life can throw in your path be solidified.

Welcome to the symphony of hope.

Merle Jordan, ThD
Emeritus Professor of Pastoral Psychology
Boston University, School of Theology

Acknowledgments

IN ANY SYMPHONY, EACH performer and instrument is vital to the sound of the performance. However, there is invariably one instrumentalist whose sound is that which blends all others into harmony. And this manuscript is certainly no exception.

In the person of Dr. Merle Jordan there is to be seen and heard one that is not only directed and connected to the various sounds written by the author. As a former professor and doctoral advisor, Dr. Jordan has encouraged this writer not only regarding his manuscript creation, but taken a personal interest in his life and professional activity. His personal interest has made this symphony of hope possible.

However, as noted, there are many instruments needed to affect the projected sound. And at this point it is impossible to choose any certain performer in the symphony. In essence, there is the collective wisdom of many former teachers and colleagues who have given this writer concepts and discoveries that have been incorporated into this manuscript. And for this I am thankful for knowledge drawn from many sources. It is a collective sound and insight that have given this writer the content of the symphony. Yet, sources must come from the available channels such as libraries, books, lectures, journals, etc. And for this I owe a debt of gratitude to Carla Birkhimer of the Trinity Seminary Library. Her expertise and patience in securing former journals, etc., for this writer to explore and re-explore as editions for the manuscript.

But all study and writing must culminate in a visible and harmonious manuscript. And for this I wish to thank Phyllis Fetzer, who sorted out the writer's scrawled handwriting into readable print. But then would come the need to correlate and symphonize the printed portion into a manuscript acceptable to any publisher. Thus was in the person of Robin Dillon, former high school English teacher and ministerial candidate who organized this work. And once more a special person was found in the person of Karen Gee, also an MTSO employee. Her insight and patience of this work is so special. No, I cannot list all who are vital in the completion of this work, but I can and must note that my last two pastoral appointments, the Brookville Port Barnett UMC and Meade Chapel UMC have been and remain my inspiration as churches that have loved and shared their love with my family and myself. Sometimes resources are found not in immediate participants of a symphony but those who work behind the scenes become an insatiable value for the total sound. It was in the person of a close friend and neighbor, Bill Fullerton, with his superior skills and expertise, enabled the mechanics of this work to succeed.

The past is so very important, but the present is that which was the past and opens a door for the future. Dr. Frank Luchsinger and the Rev. Cary Simonton, are my most recent pastors and friends. As the late Henry Nouwen notes, a pastor may be with more people than anyone in town but may be the loneliest. For the fellowship of these individuals I give my deepest thanks from a fellow traveler in the ministry of Jesus Christ.

Many sounds have been heard and experienced by this writer. It is hoped that the ultimate sound of hope proclaimed by the living, risen Christ will be that which will be heard by those who experience the symphony of hope.

Prelude

AN ADULT IN LATE mid-life, with life's twilight so close, awaits the result of recent medical tests. And from within this person breathes a question from the silent recesses of the heart and mind. "Is there any hope? Or am I destined for that state of 'non-being,' death, for becoming just another statistic in the obituaries?" And the pain of loneliness in a crowded waiting room is permeated with fear and is so very real. In a world exceedingly full of scientific advances, and yet so empty of meaning and a sense of destiny, the individual listens for the sound of hope. Yes, hope that this life can continue longer and that one's destiny can be fulfilled—or if this life is soon to end, that there is hope beyond it.

It is to such persons in a world so bereft of hope, that this word of hope must be heard . . . even above the sounds of fear and hate that seem to dominate the landscape of today. And just as individuals of later years await a sound of hope, so too does the teenager, whether in a ghetto or from a house and family of affluence. From the inner being of persons of all ages, the question sounds clearly, "Where has hope gone . . . if there was any hope to begin with?" But what has gone? What is hope? Its essence has many foci. In its more elemental state, it is that which opens up "another way," a new horizon, and that which stimulates the sense of "the new." Hope is not an irrelevant escape or fantasy, but the very basis of achievement in life itself.

"Is there anyone to reach out for me in my loneliness and in my sense of hopelessness? And the question continues to reverberate as we look and listen to the "sounds of silence," so poignantly named by the voices of the sixties. The world is waiting to hear sounds of hope for today and for the tomorrow some fear may never come!

But what is hope? It is that which tells us that "this" is not "all," that there is another way. Hope is the element that opens up the new—the horizon of fulfillment and progress.

Chapter 1

Sounds of Hope: Present and Future

INTO THE WORLD OF today, as that of yesterday, the future projects not only uncertainty regarding what tomorrow will be like, but also whether there will be a tomorrow. Yet deep within individuals lies a hope that a spark will be ignited amidst the darkness of a world so tuned for hopelessness. Is it possible that there can be meaning and hope, even if on a distant horizon, in a world that quite simply cannot understand? Can there be hope in a world clouded by the fog of despair?

To explore the dynamics of hope is to find the ever present fact that life itself is based on hope. From the mundane to the complex, sounds of hope are heard but too often are muffled by sounds of despair. And a world so filled with pain is searching for that merry sound that will give it a new dynamic to live . . . not merely exist!

For despite a world that is filled with multitudinous achievements, the haunting emptiness of hope and purpose seems too difficult to fill, and because of this need, hope has become an element to be purchased. How and why? Because whenever and wherever a hurting individual visits a therapist or other of the medical or helping professions, a purchase is enacted. And only real hope can begin to heal or alleviate the pain, the meaninglessness of life. But is this purchase expensive? Yes. For whether the one seeking hope must pay monetarily, those who are in this search for hope must invest their all. To hope is to choose, and what one chooses is to project value . . . the value of oneself and one's future.

We live in a society that is almost afraid to hope, to reach, to believe that there is another way. And while many accept hope as the key, this key is often locked away in past images and containers filled with hope never really loosed! For whether that seeker of hope is an adherent to the Christian faith, or any faith, only a vibrant, active hope can initiate the "other way."

In a world of collective entities where so many individuals feel lost in the impersonal, hope for the "one" would seem incomprehensible. And once more the picture of a contemporary human being who feels that one does not count is flashed on the screen of human experience. Is hope an avenue to reality and meaning, or merely an idle wish in a meaningless world? Once more the poignant question is spoken either overtly or silently. Are there any sounds of hope in a discordant world? And if so, where are they coming from?

Theologians and psychologists have begun to speak to a new (though very old) hope. And, it is not only those in the field of theology and psychotherapy who have discovered hope, but those in the medical field as well. Recent empirical studies in the area of psycho-immunology have shown that hope has made the very difference between life and death. Contemporary physicians like Carl Simonton, Bernie Siegel, the late Norman Cousins, and other colleagues are becoming increasingly cognizant of the validity and necessity of hope for life in its holistic perspective. No longer is it unfashionable to correlate and initiate physical and psychological factors in the healing process, but now practitioners have begun to involve the spiritual element as well!

To a world that seems to live with the "broken sentences" of life, a word of completeness must speak. And that word, the word of hope, can only come from one who was, is, and will ever be the incarnation of hope: the risen Lord. The world is waiting to hear this ultimate sound of hope that speaks to the present yet offers assurance that we are part of an eternal reality.

To envision a world of hope and to become participants in the building of this new kingdom, one must tune in to hear the sounds of hope from both the present and the future. Too often the extreme concern with the present stifles the sound of a future, a future filled with hope, a future that is fulfilled because of our present relationship with that which is eternal. That oft ignored or forgotten one designated as the "today person" is yet one seeking relationships with not only the present but also the future. We are part of a collective aggregate in the "now" of our life, but to have a future that leaves one as only a memory in society is not enough for a thinking person. And that aggregate is a group of individuals who are on a personal quest—a quest to be. In a world conditioned by ever increasing motif of hopelessness, each person either overtly or implicitly is seeking an answer to life's brevity. And living—or simply existing—in the confines of this brevity, the awesome sense of nonbeing, is ever present. The quest to be is a never-ending quest, satisfied only when real meaning is found. The individual person desires not only to be a functioning part of today's society, but also is inculcated within a sense of the "more," a future beyond one's limited years. The fear, the creepy apprehension of becoming just "another statistic" in the obituary as a final note is always present. The late theologian Paul Tillich's description of the modern human situation as "Existential Loneliness" is relevant, and yet "modern" enough even for our post-modern era. To encounter not only contemporary as well as recent and past theologians, but to hear affirmation of hope from such contemporary psychologists as Robert Emmons and Richard Cox regarding the necessity of the spirit, is to become aware of a new "symphony of hope" being written. And the writers of the symphony of hope are ever increasingly tuned to the sense of the spiritual as a valid sound, as well as the more obvious and often louder sounds from the world of the "concrete."

Our world of today, as the one of both yesterday and tomorrow, is seeking holistic truths, but often such "truths" are isolated from various fields of knowledge. And while the sounds of hope are needed from our present and waited for in the future, the major sounds are ones of violence and despair, emitted not only from the visible sources of despair, but from many that attempt to label themselves as "religion." The cancer of hate and a proclivity to destroy others are as much in evidence among so-called Christian nations as non-Christian ones. And this from those who profess to be followers of the Christ, the Prince of Peace! When we read the daily papers and watch TV, the fact of good news is sparse in quantity. Are there sounds of hope from the present and future? Yes! But there must be a revolutionary move toward accepting the fact that our hope is not in the concrete, the visible alone, but in the reality of the spirit if we can hear sounds of hope amidst the sounds of despair in a cacophony of violence.

We live in two worlds whether this fact is admitted by those who think they exist in one world or by those who accept a "two world" life. While Albert Einstein (and others before his emergence in the areas of math and science) opens the "secret" of physics to a totally new view and perspective, his discovery would verify what open-minded thinkers have always implied, if not openly verbalized. Life is *more* than the visible. The reality of the spirit, the unseen, the mystery, is and has been ever before us. Similarly, in the solid denial of theologians such as Gordon Kaufman of Harvard Divinity School, who affirm that there is no evidence of life after death, such affirmation projects a closed mind-set, Happily there are authorities in both fields of science and religion who, with a growing number of others with like minds, dare to affirm a two-world reality of life. It is this writer's contention that a hurting world that is orientated to hopelessness can only find itself if and when a real theology and a psychology of hope are validated.

The overt and implicit call for hope cannot be ignored if our world of today is to find itself, its purpose, its ultimate goals and fulfillment. To read the daily articles in our newspapers is to see the confusion and fear that permeate all of life. Yet while we expect to see and hear the everyday bad news, the real contradiction is to see and hear the so-called purveyors of hope, the Christian faith participants, give credence, acceptance, and agreement with the method of violence and negation of love. And this emanating from a society built on love that centuries ago was known by "how they loved one another!" It is to such a panorama of contradiction that the revolutionary dynamics of hope proposes to enter a new sound and yet one voiced by the creator at the beginning of time. There can be, and there is, the reality of a new sound, a sound not composed on the scale of hopelessness and the minor key of despair, but one transposed into a major sound of hope of love in action.

To encounter a real and scientifically respectable hope is not to negate the scientific or the area of theology, but to see and listen to the new sound of hope experienced by participants in both areas of knowledge.

Vignettes of how hope makes a difference in life, both subjectively and objectively, are becoming more frequent. And while the elements of hope are becoming more empirically verifiable, the fact remains that there must be a correlative acceptance of the value of both areas of reality. In essence, then, it would appear that the real and inclusive answer to the hurts of the world must be played out on the real life stage by blending these sounds into a harmonious performance of past and present to project a new future and to hear a symphony of hope.

A new future is one that arises from an acceptance of what is really real and is called for from our world of today and yesterday. The sounds of hope have, and continue to have, a sense of listening from the past and the present in order to build the new future. As noted in my previous work, "real hope must be an active hope, not one of the passive variety."[1]

It is to the contemporary sound of hopelessness and despair that a psychology and theology of hope must speak. The foreboding fear of imminent destruction, either by terrorists or a breakdown in our society, is fed not only as the society beyond the church as such, but by those deemed "Christian," even those affirming they are "born again." One must ask without being satirical or sarcastic, "what are they reborn for?" As Polkinghorne and Welker have projected in their book, *The End of the World and the Ends of God*, the collision between the finite and the infinite is clearly set forth. Either we are on a collision course with extinction as our end, or we accept God's end as a new beginning.[2] Today our world waits for a new beginning.

As we hear the sounds of hope sounded by writers such as Polkinghorne and Welker, we begin to see the future of God's plan, a plan envisioned by those who accept the promise of hope. A world tired of broken promises awaits a verifiable promise based on historical reality, which became alive in the present with anticipation of a new future. Only by hearing sounds of hope can these goals be seen and heard in our uniqueness and in our relationship with the universe.

This unique relationship has been and continues to be set forth by such incisive writers as the late James Loder when he states:

> If we turn to the sciences, it will be evident that the human spirit reaches into the depths and unto the outer limits of the universe and beyond. The final result of such exploration remains beyond our grasp, but there are important analogies between the exocentric dynamics of the human spirit and the expanding universe.[3]

Our culture and the world in which it functions projects the theme of unhope in multiple areas. From the torn aspects of a society in almost constant conflict—social, political, personal, and religious—hope is clouded by the fog that creates unhope, a fog that seems to increase in these areas and every area of concern.

To envision hope in such a scene, there must come a wind from the beyond to drive this fog away. As we look through the fog of degradation,

1. Janacek, *Theology and Psychology of Hope*, 6.
2. Polkinghorne and Welker, eds., *End of the World*, 5.
3. Loder, *The Logic of the Spirit*, 6.

only the fresh air of the resurrection projects hope. For amidst the past failure of a world permeated by darkness and death, one came from beyond in the person of the risen Christ. And suddenly the scene began to change. Life has arrived! The worship of the past and the present, with their focus on only the now, sees and welcomes the future, the new.

Chapter 2

Sounds of Hope Being Heard

CONTEMPORARY PSYCHOLOGY HAS SHOWN us an increasing interest in hope as a valid factor for a healthy life. Human beings are designed to hope, and this is their essential question in life. As Arthur Burton noted in his work *Interpersonal Psychotherapy*, "without hope no treatment can proceed."[1]

Viktor Frankl, a survivor of the Holocaust, found meaning even in the unthinkable horrors of Auschwitz, giving us the dynamics of logo-therapy (existential analysis). Meanwhile, theologians of the latter part of the twentieth century have rediscovered that something or someone gives meaning to life. It is with this age, so permeated with existential anxiety, that this work is concerned. As the late Paul Tillich so incisively notes, "religion is that which is one's ultimate concern."[2] Robert Emmons in his groundbreaking work, *The Psychology of Ultimate Concerns*, reaffirms this poignant truth for our present situation.[3] For Emmons and other like-minded scholars, spirituality and religion are *not* to be isolated from the world of theology and philosophy, nor from the world of science.

It has been, and continues to be, this writer's intent to correlate the riches of logotherapy with the dynamics of hope, ever cognizant of the need to dialogue with the scientific community. If eschatology is to be seen as more than a sojourn into a "theology of science fiction," it must not avoid, nor waiver, from its dialogue with not only contemporary psychology, but with the scientific community as well. Despite fears from too many in the religious realm, and a possible disdain by closed-minded scientists, in reality there should be no real conflict if and when both areas

1. Burton, *Interpersonal Psychotheraphy*, 134.
2. Tillich, *The New Being*, 6.
3. Emmons, *The Psychology of Ultimate Concerns*, 4–5.

initiate true dialogue and find empirical truth. In any quest for truth and the new, there must be no apprehensiveness regarding empirical studies and those of the spiritual that in their respective areas dare to be open to new views, not merely revisions of a past conflict.

Our world, though almost constantly in a state of transition, has nevertheless perpetuated self-sabotage by not seeing or hearing reality as a whole. All too frequently the material and spiritual are seen and heard as separate entities, despite increasing studies that see the holistic pattern of life, from the most minute to the farthest reaches of outer space. Life is an organism. Each part is to be that which functions within the whole. From the laboratory scientist who deals with the microcosmic to the cosmologist exploring the "beyond," there is an increasing reverence for the creative pattern and design of what we term "reality." Since the breakthrough of Einstein's theory, to the work (and we shall explore some of his work later) of Brian Green and Polkinghorne and Welker, life and purpose are hearing new "sounds of hope." With a world that all too often seems to be hearing only sounds of hate and violence, even in the name of the Prince of Peace, this hope cannot be heard too soon!

In contrast to the extremists on both ends of the theological spectrum, sounds of hope are also coming from a renewed interest in that oft-described term "soul." The term "soul" used (and misused) is no longer put on the shelf of pre-modernity. Writers in the field of psychology of religion no longer project fear or apprehension when discussing that oft mysterious element of human being designated as "soul." Yes, that intangible is once more becoming the "in" element in a world once so dominated by the concrete—the here and now.

While it is relevant to speak of "soul" and the future, all too often this is left to the right wings of theology who thrive on (and profit from) a fear-based society. The plethora of books telling of end times and the end of the world seem to reign in so-called Christian bookstores and even Walmart! A world so filled with apprehension and fear of the future (including a wrathful God) is a prime target for such prophets of doom. A world so in need of hope, and the sound of a living hope, too often hears such a desecration of what passes for Christianity.

It is to the extreme of the right and the archaic revival of old heresies that a real sound of hope is needed. Moltmann and others have sounded their note of hope and proclaim the exciting truth that what the world mistakenly calls the end is in God's plan a new beginning. It is with this new beginning that we will begin to hear sounds of a symphony of hope, a symphony that the world has been waiting too long to hear. This symphony will need not only those who compose the harmony, but also those who will become participants, or "players," in a "symphony of hope."

As Moltmann and others have reinitiated a sense of hope where previous individuals from both the right and left have projected a future of despair (except for a few who follow narrow fundamentalism), the fact that God is coming with hope, real hope, is an exciting change. In Moltmann's award-winning book, *The Coming of God*, there has come a new openness to eschatology, a word too often relegated to a closed fundamentalist mentality but that is now "in" both to contemporary theology and for persons of science. In fact, it is now a focal point in some of the academy's most sophisticated conference of professionals from the areas of theology, psychology, and science. How refreshing to see a holistic approach in a world that is broken in many ways. The reality of "living in two worlds" is now a valid element in contemporary theology and the world of science. A vacuum that existed erroneously between what was really real and the "supposed world of metaphysical imagination" is becoming increasingly non-existent.

In reality, it is becoming increasingly evident that those not only in the fields of theology and psychology but also science are admitting their own lack of ultimate knowledge. The once almost smug attitude of some so-called scientists is greatly diminished as the vastness, and yet interrelatedness, of our world and the universe are being explored. Even as one begins to "see" the incomprehensible regarding size, the statement of the late Albert Einstein gives us a written "clue" to its understanding, as he once noted, "the incomprehensible of the universe is the fact that it *is* comprehensible." To individuals on this small, yet not insignificant, planet Earth, there comes a new sense that we need not live nor just exist in a state of "astronomical intimidation," but that we do count. As the late Jim Loder noted so incisively in one of his last books, the very fact that we can comprehend in part even the unfathomable reality of the multitudinous universe gives us a hint of our interrelatedness with the "beyond." In essence, whether one looks at reality as an incomprehensible vastness or in a view of it in its microcosmic state, there is a definite connection.[4] As my mentor Dr. Merle Jordan has noted, the last fifty years has seen a dramatic and dynamic change in how the theological aspects of reality

4. Loder, *The Logic of the Spirit*, 6.

are now accepted as compared to a few decades ago. In fact without being overly optimistic, the future need and rise of theology in psychology will in essence be seen as clinical theology. Whatever one envisions or sees as something beyond the concrete, beyond the visual, whether one is a believer, an agnostic, or an atheist, there is a call to hear sounds of something more—in other words, an awareness of the spirit.

In reality, psychology and theology have been "long-time associates if not accepted relatives."[5] However, as one surveys the last fifty years there is an increasing awareness of the need for both fields to draw on the resources of each other to accommodate the needs of the human being, whether believers or not. The once fragmented fields are now becoming more in tune with each other and exuding valid sounds of hope—sounds that can and will answer the silent cries for help in a hurting world. John Polkinghorne, the eminent physicist/priest of Cambridge has noted that we are only on the threshold of knowledge regarding that entity called the human being.[6] All too often in the past, participants in both the fields of theology and science have constructed barriers between the two areas of knowledge. Hurting individuals who reach for and need answers from both areas of study are left with fragments of life in place of a holistic source from which to draw meaning and fulfillment of life. As a theologian noted decades ago, "Theologians and biblical scholars are answering questions that no one has asked," noting the irrelevance of much that passes for religious studies.[7] As with the physical sciences, so too, in the field of psychology, one can see and hear answers to life that are either empty or irrelevant.

In a recent editorial in the *Journal of Religion and Health,* David Learing incisively notes that the field of Psychology of Religion may be of paramount importance in dealing with personal tragedy. This is only validated by the living human documents who have found and who continue to find meaning for the person who loses "all" unless there is that other world. Describing the earlier loss of a student colleague, Learing affirmed the need for answers. Too frequently, though, the only "answers" are continued notes of despair and acts of violence regarding human rights in the name of religion.

5. Merle Jordan, lecture, "Conference on Spirituality," Boston, 1998.
6. Polkinghorne and Welker, eds. *The End of the World,* 31.
7. Harvey Potthoff, lecture at Iliff School of Theology, Denver, 1962.

A world caught up in the return to violence has once more forgotten the essence, the value of life as its individuals and societies (including our own America) revert to such actions. And the press for peace continues via the violence that is our "peaceful" response! An oft repeated phrase from returning soldiers is, "We have met the enemy and he is us." While this was a quote from a movie regarding the Vietnam War, it is relevant in our present situation. Is there an answer to the world's almost perpetual fascination with hate and conflict? Yes! But only if and when we begin to recognize and move from a theology and psychology of despair into a theology and psychology of hope. Only with a vision of a new world played out on the screen of reality, while building a symphony of hope, will this new world be affected. As noted previously, and a theme that will echo throughout this work: the world awaits sounds of hope, sounds that have already reverberated across the centuries, when the one who came from beyond broke the hopelessness of death and affirmed, "I am alive forevermore." "I am the resurrection and the life." The ultimate night of hopelessness has passed, the dirge of gloom is not the final sound, because there is the sound of hope coming from beyond, and yet is very near as we listen—listen for the quiet sound that stirs within us.

Is such a belief merely a hopeful affirmation of faith, and could this have any hints of verification in the world of science and medicine where incomprehensible advances are taking place? Yes, for as medicine has found new cures and treatments that were once thought to be impossible, it is here that hope and its dynamics once more have shown the way. The difference that hope has initiated with new medical advances is being found by solid empirical research because, in reality, every scientific advance began because of a "hope" regarding its achievement.

Quoting Einstein and the new vision now becoming prominent, Reading notes, "The opinion prevailed among advanced minds that it was time that belief should be replaced increasingly by knowledge; belief that did not itself rest on knowledge was superstition, and as such had to be opposed . . . the scientific method can teach us nothing else beyond how facts are related to and conditioned by each other ... [S]cience without religion is lame; religion without science is blind."[8]

To encounter a real and scientifically respectable hope is not to negate the scientific of the area of theology, but to see and listen to the new sound of hope experienced by participants in both areas of knowledge.

8. Reading, *Hope and Despair*, 132.

Vignettes of how hope makes a difference in life both subjectively and objectively are becoming more frequent. While the elements of hope are becoming more empirically verifiable, the fact remains that there must be a correlative acceptance of the value of both areas of reality. In essence, then, it would appear that the real and inclusive answer to the hurts of the world must be played out on the real stage of life by blending these sounds into a harmonious performance of past and present to project a new future and to hear a symphony of hope.

A new future is a future that arises from an acceptance of what is really real and is called for from our world of today and of yesterday. The sounds of hope have and continue to have a sense of listening from the past and the present in order to build the new future. As noted in a previous work, "real hope must be an active hope, not one of the passive variety."[9] Tragically the seeming popularity of the concern for the future has been absorbed and taken advantage of by the radical right who simply proclaim doom for all except for the "chosen few" in the LaHaye and Jenkins camp. Partially due to the reaction from unknowledgeable "experts on prophecy," the extreme left has negated this very reality and the possibility of a valid eschatology, proclaiming a hopeless future. Thus the only future is one of a hopeless world spiraling into nothingness!

Out of the fires of hate and despair in World War II and its sounds of death and destruction, a theologian of the stature of Moltmann had struck a new note of hope, of life and future, of God's plan for a new world waiting to be born. In brilliant contrast to so much of a theology of despair, the confidence of a community of resurrection was now to be seen. A new world, a world where life lives not only in memory or collectively, for everyone individually, was now a living certainty! The sounds of hope were no longer muffled by the tones of skepticism from the skeptical left nor the hate and despairing sounds of a decadent right wing fundamentalism. Life and love were now becoming the new "in." Individuals who were becoming tired of, but accustomed to, almost perpetual sounds of hopelessness and despair began to tune in to a "station of hope" and hear sounds of hope in its major key. And this "station of hope" was first "on the air" broadcasting the news of resurrection from a tomb of death and despair with the risen Christ as the anchorman proclaiming sounds of hope!

9. Janacek, *A Theology and Psychology of Hope*, 132.

Chapter 3

Sounds of Hope: Dynamics and Impact

OUR WORLD HEARS A multiplicity of sounds. Sounds of despair and hope are in constant collision and yet have elements in common. In essence, each is defined by the other, for one cannot really define despair without admitting its opposition. And thus with hope. Until one admits the existence and possibility of despair, hope cannot be defined. Perhaps a relevant illustration of hope being defined was thrust upon me years ago when I was expressing my doctoral thesis oral examination. After I had presented my dissertation on hope, one of my examiners asked a very clear and relevant question, "Bob, can you define hope for us?" Suddenly all of my hours of research and writing seemed to be in vain until my answer proved to be what really was at least an attempt at a definition: "Dr. Godfrey, I'd rather have it than be able to define it."[1] In reality hope must become a part of us and its definition is best expressed by its actions.

To define hope and to explore its dynamic is to accept at least its possibility and then, in an existential level of faith, reach for it. It must be noted and affirmed that the concept of hope is not a new element either in theology or psychology. In fact, life itself is lived on the basis of hope and hope's dialogue with its opposite, despair. In everyday living the word is used almost daily as we hear, "I hope I'm on time," "I hope life improves," "I hope my life is extended," etc.

However, hope's real dynamic is one that serves as a thrust to and for any creative endeavor. From the laboratory scholar to the most unskilled laborer, hope is a factor, in fact, *the* factor in the "how" of any achievement from the most simple to the most complicated. While the sounds of hope may not be auditory, deep within all who seek to build and create,

1. Robert Janacek, Boston University, September 11, 2001

there are sounds of hope, i.e., "Can this really work?" etc. Desmond Tutu said, "Hope is not a new innovation. In fact, it is the essence of the 'not yet.' And hope is not the solid domain of the theologians nor of those in the healing profession, both physical and psychological. Hope is to be found wherever and whenever a conscious being is interacting with her or his environment."[2] Today, as our yesterdays, the sounds of hope are being heard—if ever so faintly—as a wounded world desperate to hear if this word can be translated into reality and life!

Bishop Tutu, who spoke of hope after years of persecution, noted "God is transforming the world now—through us—because God loves us . . . Some will say that this view is 'optimistic,' but I am not an optimist. Optimism relies on appearances and very quickly turns into pessimism when the appearances change. I see myself as a realist, and the vision of hope I want to offer you in this book is based on reality—the reality I have seen and lived."[3] Thus one cannot live without making a choice, for there is no such element in life as total neutrality. It would seem that even the one who disparages hope has a "hope" that there is no hope!

In a world that is so blatantly skeptical of an absolute, the very concept of hope as noted would be relegated to being an icon of the past, especially in a post-modern society. Nevertheless, while advocates of post-modernism may revel in the new world of no absolutes, nor verified truth, at the same time they are self-contradicting their philosophy. If, as a postmodernist would say, "There are no absolutes," are they not affirming that their belief is in essence "absolute"?

Can there be a sense of something or someone being able to give us a solid awareness that there can be some "absolute"? In reality hope must base its dynamics on affirming there is something "more." As Moltmann's well-known statement about hope asserts, hope tells us there is another way! When this affirmation is accepted, the "hope" for answers to life's purpose and meaning becomes a real possibility. It is encouraging, even in these times of violence fueled by hate and a desecration of what was once the realm of the holy, that there are quiet sounds of hope being heard and acted upon. For despite the mass "sell out" of what was once a theology of love to a reorientation toward a mentality of patriotic violence, there are signals of hope. Whereas the essential code of many liberals was

2. *God Has a Dream*, 15.
3. Ibid., vii.

to be liberal in anything but a new idea, and conservatives "conserved" everything except love and compassion, there is a valid change occurring.

At Boston University and other academic institutions like Duke University, it is no longer archaic or unfashionable to speak of the spiritual. For example, Boston University has held conferences on spirituality while schools like Duke now have funded chairs of Evangelism. Schools that were once extremely conservative halls of learning, such as Eastern Baptist Theological Seminary, have social activists of the caliber of Ron Sider and Tony Campolo. The "either/or" pattern of psychology and theology is no longer the general motif. Bridges between the two areas, though still infrequent, are being constructed.

Theologians of the stature of Carl Bratten, Leonard Sweet, and the continental theologians, e.g., Moltmann and Pannenberg, are affirming hope in this age of despair. While theologians are becoming increasingly hopeful of a future, psychologists such as Orlo Strunk, Richard Cox, M. Jordan, Ken Pargant, and Robert Emmons are carving new highways of thought on the once barren road to despair. A world that has experienced a holocaust, along with multiple wars large and small, would seemingly be ready for hope. But tragically true is the fact that, as in previous centuries, what passes for religion, let alone Christianity, is contributing to hopelessness by joining forces of vengeance, violence, and persecution in the name of God!

Nevertheless this writer is still unwavering in the belief that there is hope that life is not spiraling in an unstoppable descent. How? Why? It is my contention and affirmation, based not only on feelings of optimism but on historical and scientific reality, that there is a master conductor—a conductor who will not force participants to play in harmony, but who waits for the most "imperfect applicants" to join in a "symphony of hope." And how a world so bereft of the music of the sound of hope waits to hear such harmony!

This need to harmonize and to synthesize the ambiguities in life is perpetual. To see and hear despair in so much of life is to be tempted to be overcome by negation. Anthony Reading in his recent treatise entitled *Hope and Despair* speaks a relevant and hopeful word to the situation:

> Our ability to hope and predict the future is a two edged sword. If we can see good times ahead as we peer into the crystal ball, we generate hope and energy. But if what we see is dark and foreboding we become weighed down with inactivity and despair . . . hope

> gives us only possibilities, not guarantees, but mobilizes us to act
> to analyze and understand our problems and to try to solve them.[4]

From a purely psychological viewpoint, this facing of the reality of many uncertainties is accurate, but our concern and quest at this point of exploration utilizes the revolutionary dynamic of hope. This hope is a hope beyond finite limitations based on a new future, as Braaten noted in 1969 in his book, *The Future of God.*

In a world that undeniably focuses on the power of human inquiry and finds its answer in violence, whether from the secular world or from what is erroneously seen as "Christian" religion, hope does seem to be missing. In fact, it could be labeled or put on a shelf of the past as an inert element in the "laboratory of real life." Thus despair and its resulting hopelessness and evil have been released by religions of multiple types, including what is labeled Christianity. The Pandora's box story shows that after all evil escapes into our world and would contaminate all of life, only one element remains: hope. For when all the demons had flown out to do their duties of hate and disaster (presently, often under the mute flag of Christianity, as well as the more easily labeled pagan faith), the only element left was hope.[5]

It is our contention that real hope is a valid reality and, in essence, is non-negotiable if and when we are to hear the sounding of its source: the creator of the universe and our master conductor. Psychology, theology, and science are not in opposition if and when each recognizes the validity and integrity of each field upon the other. While numerous attempts at hope have been made to integrate and/or correlate via journals and conferences, too often each field seems to explore the other, but then return to "their" own answer or specificity. As far back as 1982, Orlo Strunk called for a new vision in the pastoral counseling movement. As Strunk notes, "The theological question is manifested in at least two questions. Should the pastoral counselor primarily be a practicing theologian as part of his or her theological project with the technical skills of behavior rather than a counselor-psychologist who utilizes the resource of the religious community?"[6] This problem would certainly be verified not only by any

---

4. Reading, *Hope and Despair,* 172.

5. Ibid., 173.

6. Strunk, "Role of Visioning," 7.

pastoral counseling but also by the entire spectrum of psychology and theology.

All too often, as has been inferred by this writer, each area is weighted in favor of their specialty rather than blending into the total landscape of reality. Happily, hope is not an element that can be claimed (nor owned!) by either field as sole owner and proprietor. For this we can be thankful. Hope, as we have seen, is, in essence, the "not yet," while on the other side is that which proclaims there is "another way."

Because there is another way, the "not yet" can be an avenue for new fulfillment in life: a life of hope unceasing. For while there is a wide divergence of views regarding eschatological fulfillment, the one dominating theme projected by the liberal, conservative, fundamentalist, and more recently the theologians of hope, the future remains paramount. Mode, methodology, and quality may greatly differ, but the terms of hope for restoration must be a constant for all. It is with this constant in mind that the element of hope in both its theological and psychological dynamics must be drawn. A world that is so full of words has yet too many blank pages in the newspaper of life and continues to play minor tones of despair rather than those of hope in the major key so greatly needed. In essence, what is needed is what J. Randall Nichols wrote in his book, appropriately titled, *The Restoring Word.* While his excellent treatise was primarily focused on the area of preaching, one cannot deny nor negate the validity of the word.[7] For it was that living word in Christ who initiated hope to a lonely German prisoner of war in an internment camp, Jurgen Moltmann, and the rest is history. This word, as Moltmann noted, restored the prisoner from death to life. The word was acted upon and hope was reborn!

Sounds of hope may occur in a multiplicity of situations and from varied sources. A sound of hope may be heard as one listens to "the sounds of silence." As many writers whose focus is on the inner spirit, such as the late Henry Nouwen, Carlos Caretta, and the contemporary professor of spirituality at Columbia Seminary, Ben Campbell Johnson, have noted, the need to "listen" in silence is very important. In our noisy and action-driven society, this listening is certainly a rarity. To the one seemingly entrapped in a so-called hopeless situation, the sound may come via the word of one who once expressed the death of hope but now can empathetically reach out to the one in need. For even as we read almost endless

---

7. Nichols, *The Restoring Word.*

accounts of pain, despair, and death, there may be the sound of another who speaks out of the mystery of existence to the one that really listens for the word of hope.

As Ben Campbell Johnson so vividly noted, it is possible to hear sounds within one's very being that cannot be recorded nor comprehended by human sensory faculties.[8] While the "concrete only" mindset may easily dismiss such "spiritual wanderings," the fact remains that even the most secular concrete-oriented person within the laboratory of the physical must admit that there is something beyond the visible, the material, that allows one's mind to tune in beneath the surface of thought. The ordinary is not really ordinary, and the now of our lives is not the all of human experience.

In this chapter, our exploration of sounds of hope will not be confined to just the secular or the spiritual, but rather in a comprehensive symphonic approach. Yet in a sense this may be self-contradictory, in that the total picture of hope and of life itself has no line of demarcation, for from the most ancient experiences of the spirit to modern physics, there has and continues to be a sense of the whole, the holistic view of life. It is our purpose to project a holistic approach to hope in its theory, its practice, and its essential dynamics, for to hope is to see that always there is another way. This way is not and cannot be confined to either the visible or the invisible. The God whom we worship is certainly spiritual but was shown and expressed most clearly by the incarnation, in everyday life as the risen Christ and his continued presence.

It is refreshing to explore and experience the literature of today, which is increasingly cognizant of both the spiritual and the secular. Whereas this field was almost off-limits to the empirical mind, such is no longer the case. Spirituality is not only "in" but is beginning to enter areas once thought to be off-limits. Not only are the medical and scientific fields making spirituality fashionable but even the media is. Yet this in itself, however encouraging the sounds may be, is not the total picture or sound. In fact it is popular to affirm that one is spiritual without the hindrance of really believing or focusing on any certainty of belief or doctrine.

Nevertheless, the fact that the media and its constituency are once more speaking of spirituality does add a hopeful aspect to the

8. Johnson, *Living Before God*, 55.

contemporary scene. The once closed off world of the concrete, the material, is now opening itself to something or even someone beyond and/or beneath the surface of human experience. This writer will never forget the statement by Dr. John Dixon Copp of Boston University in a seminar on mysticism when he said, "the more we become aware, the closer we are to reality."[9] Certainly this is the all-encompassed need. Reality must be tuned in if we are to hear and experience more of life. In a world whose very surface is built on power and violence, even by those labeled Christians, a cognizance of the spirit of wonder is all too infrequent. And yet the quest for hope must be pursued.

A distant sound of encouragement and hope was heard in an article by Sang Uk Lee in the recent *Journal of Religion and Health*. He noted that the Weltanschauung of even the most blatant atheist such as Freud, but also the early psychologists of religion, William James along with Paul Ricoeur, and poets are converging in seeing the world where everything is a part of the whole.[10] Certainly in our broken society and world as a whole, a holistic approach cannot come too soon!

Could it be that even Freud in his use of essential depth psychology was possibly hoping for a better worldview? Could he have real hope, if presented with a more valid and relevant theology, as opposed to an oppressive one like as he expressed? After all, hope is not limited to those with whom we agree. As my college professor of philosophy, the late Dr. Wilbur Mullen, so avidly noted, "Truth is truth if the devil himself says so!"[11]

All too frequently we may fail to hear calls for hope from the most unlikely, but so needed source. To see beyond our human limitation is imperative if real hope is to be grasped and enacted in life.

Our world calls out for hope in every area, for unless this is heard, no real value can be experienced. It is, in essence, the dynamics that enable any goal to be achieved. In a world so permeated with a closed-minded view both politically and religiously, real hope would appear to be too often an "idle wish in a harsh unbending world." But now we are

9. John Dixon Copp, seminar on the Psychology of Mysticism, Boston University School of Theology, 1955.

10. Lee, "Constructing an Aesthetic Weltanschauung: Freud, James, and Ricoeur," 273.

11. Wilber Mullen, lecture, Introduction to Philosophy, Eastern Nazarene College, 1949.

beginning to hear sounds of a new symphony of hope beginning to be composed. To the embarrassment of what passes for religion—even that labeled evangelical—sounds of hope are being literally heard by the rock and popular music of our day. Benefit concerts to help the poor and forgotten are becoming more frequent and greater in number. Meanwhile, too many supposed followers of the risen Christ are more concerned with business profit via war and the persecution of the unwanted, and they only utter prayers for the less fortunate. A so-called "Christian" nation such as ours may hold prayer breakfasts without hearing the call of the hungry and thirsty. I wonder what hope for others is in their prayers? Or are the prayers spoken not really prayed to God but to power?

Perhaps such irrelevant sounds are being heard from the religious right who exert effort at understanding the last day via arguments regarding the rapture, etc. Even the liberal area of religion, which too often is hope only for social change, seems to muffle the real sounds of hope. For these sounds, as noted, may come from the most unlikely sources. Doesn't that sound like early Christianity and even the Christ who didn't fit the religious mold of the day? It is becoming increasingly evident that new sounds are needed. These sounds must come from this primary source: the one who created hope, the living Lord. But the sounds of hope are not limited to a certain few who have all the answers regarding the "what, why, and wherefore" of true religion. The muffled sounds of hope are emanating from those who believe in hope, yet too often fail to become active proponents of hope. Hope, in its true definition and expression, must not be passive, but must be that which activates the whole of life, both personally and collectively.

Our concern in initiating the valid sound of hope must be ever cognizant of a hope that speaks and acts against the mode of both the left and the right, neither of which really takes seriously the dynamic changes in both theology and psychology. Likewise hope must speak and act against the constant depiction of violence and despair being enacted by both affirming and non-affirming adherents of religion. We have the two extremes. The right wing of religion continues to focus on the end time, which in essence is an ending of all hope except for those whose beliefs blends with their own, while the religious left seems to be left with only human hope for a better world—if that world survives at all!

While multiple works continue to flood the Christian and non-Christian bookstores, there are writers who have exposed the heresy of the rapture. For these individuals, hope is the basis of revelation. None-theless, the majority of even middle-of-the-road evangelicals accept the rapture as valid truth; it is a common heresy. Too often due to such abuses of scripture, contemporary liberals have negated the whole concept of es-chatology as an icon of the past or a belief of non-intellectuals.

However, eschatology is the true goal, the dynamic of all true re-ligion including Christianity, which initiated the concept by the Lord of the future: the risen Christ! Moltmann and others have affirmed and continue to proclaim a theology that has its basic dynamic and goal as one that is future-oriented. A theology of the future, one much-needed today, permeates all of Moltmann's theology.

We live in the world of the present and yet we know in deeper mo-ments that all is in no way the present, that life is fluid and always in motion with the future calling us. In fact, even during our sleep there are sounds, most of which we seem unable to hear and decipher. But the tragic fact is, as Ben Campbell Johnson has noted, that too many sup-posedly intellectual people go through life in a state of "life-sleep."[12] To listen to the voices around us in every walk of life, laity and clergy alike, is to hear sounds of boredom, despair, and meaninglessness, even as we "sleep walk" through life. But if we at this juncture of life will listen for the sounds of hope, perhaps they and we will be awakened to what the creator has always had in store for creation—a life of hope and new beginning!

As this writer has explored the areas of hope from both the theology and psychology dynamics, many encouraging truths have emerged. James Jones, a philosopher of religion, including Christianity, has noted that, "It is no longer news that an increasing number of studies have found posi-tive correlations between religious beliefs and practice and mental health with longevity."[13]

This was very different and contrasting with my undergraduate days in the 1950s and even in early graduate school in the 1960s when religion was a "hidden," if not divided, element in "good psychology." In fact as a young clinician intern, I felt that my colleagues were reticent to admit their own relationship to any religious institution. And how shocking it would be to individuals of this mindset of the 1960s to see a full-scale conference at Boston University on "Spiritual Issues in Mental Health."

12. Johnson, *Living Before God*, 2.
13. Jones, "Religion, Health, and the Psychology of Religion," 317.

Certainly the limitations of psychology are changing, and hopefully for the better. Nevertheless, one must be cautioned regarding this revival of the spiritual that it not be used as the good time in the church of the 1950s. The temptation could very well be that promotion in both areas could either concede or use their movement for selfish or narrow purposes. It could be that the revival of the spiritual, and even God-talk, could develop into a situation whereby God and the spirit become tools to further a composite theology and psychology.

Over seven decades ago, the Oxford scholar J. B. Phillips wrote a small monograph entitled *Your God is Too Small*. In both the conservative and liberal constituency, this is very relevant . . . even in the twenty-first century! For while the liberal arm of Christianity dares to conform God to what they feel is relevant, the other constituency, Biblical conservatives, see God as a personal power to effect their ideology, from "Christian" standards to political choices.

Nevertheless the encouraging fact remains that "these positive effects of hope and optimism have been found to be an assurance of better health and interrelated with culture."[14] While certain cultures use standards of non-drinking, etc., those aspects of religious standards do have an overall effect on their general health. Health is in reality not merely absence of illness, but a state of balance: physical, mental, and, as is becoming increasingly more acceptable, spiritual. The sounds of hope can never be limited to the "here and now" or to the beyond. Yet the vivid fact remains that every individual does have a cognizance of "something beyond one's self" and at least a hope regarding a fulfillment of life beyond time. There the dynamic relationship and essence of a solid psychology and theology of hope cannot be dismissed or remain an irrelevant option.

As we delve more deeply into the dynamics of representation of a theology of hope, it is vital that we see not only the theological reality of hope, but also its practices in daily life. We tune now to hear more "sounds of hope" as expressed by individuals such as Moltmann and Panneberg. Before we explore the dynamic of a theology of hope, however, one vital note must be inserted as a need for "hearing a sound in harmony." Dr. Carrie Doering, formerly of Boston University and now at Iliff School of Theology, relates a story relevant to our study. She tells of a student in class, a pastoral student who was filled with anxiety upon

14. Ibid., 319.

being asked by her senior pastor to administer pastoral care to a couple within her church who had just experienced a heartbreaking miscarriage. At the moment the very "well trained" and brilliant graduate student was permeated with anxiety. Her in depth studies in the psychology of pastoral care, along with both modern and post-modern theology were of no relevant help to her. At this vital point of human need this call for hope was imperative, but the "student professor" could not understand how to link theology with praxis.

To be armed with the tools of modern scholarship was not enough, as Doering noted. However, at this point in time what was needed was an ability to relate with empathy to meet a human need. It was the moment of existential need that must be answered and called for a comforting sound of hope. The hurting couple in their loss were either overtly or implicitly calling for a positive note of hope, a sound to give some harmony in this monumental discord in their lives.

Is hope always relevant? Is it possible that to give hope in impossible situations would be an act of incompetent cruelty? No, but to answer this seeming dilemma, the sounds of hope must be seen in their relationship to all of reality, and this is never confined to a timeframe of the present. As W. Edward Farley has successfully confirmed, the good news of Jesus is announcing hope for every situation.[15] And this situation can be one where all human lives are limited. Yet in the mind of the creator there is hope—a hope that goes beyond the "nows" of our life and existence.

15. Farley, "Can Preaching Be Taught?", 177.

Chapter 4

Sounds of Hope Transposed

FROM THE EVER INSIGHTFUL and proficient writings of Howard Clinebell comes a clarion call for the need of ultimate meaning in life. Dr. Clinebell wrote:

> We human beings are creatures who hunger for some sense of ultimate meaning in our lives. We seem to be the only species who knows we will die . . . at some level of our mind (usually repressed). We know that we are ultimately alone. In the modern scientific world this painful aloneness is increased by the fear that we might be ultimately alone in the whole universe.[1]

Certainly as we absorb Dr. Clinebell's critical question and truth, the need for a vital hope becomes not only spiritually and/or theologically valid, but empirically as well. This feeling is very real in the world of our now, as greatly as in the less sophisticated past. As Clinebell further notes, we have a spiritual longing and need that we must find some way to satisfy. We need to sense that there is a spiritual reality, that there is more than our three dimensional life.[2]

While we would want to believe that the universe is basically friendly, this part of the universe called Earth seems to deny this hope.

In a world that is substantially a one-sided pseudo-religion of violence, resulting in pathos beyond comprehension, there is still the silent or overt cry for hope. Yes, hope that has either been destroyed or ignored, the hope guaranteed by its author of hope, the Christ of faith. Into this environment of despair, loneliness, and meaninglessness, there is the deplorable exhibition of a pseudo-Christianity covertly (if not always visually) verbalizing faith in its political agenda—an agenda formulated unto

1. Clinebell, "Religion Can Make You Sick or Keep You Well," 2.
2. Ibid.

the guide of "accepted" Christianity, but which is in reality a mockery of the teaching of the Prince of Peace! One must wonder if amidst this stifling of the Prince of Peace and his message there may be heard the cry of the Old Testament prophet who asked, "Is there no balm in Gilead?" But this cannot be heard above the sounds of hate, vengeance, and a pseudo-biblical shield.

At this point in our projection of the true sounds of hope, we must initiate and present the need for transposition. In the realm of music there are certain indisputable facts that must be evident if a true sound is to be heard. Each participant must play in the proper key, for to do otherwise would give the hearer or audience a sound of unimaginable discord or a cacophony of unrelated notes. In a real way this happens all too often in the fields of psychology, theology, and the sciences. While each feels they are "connecting" and/or integrating their diverse fields, too often they are present in "their key" but not transposing into a key amenable to the others. This fact of transposition was first encountered by the writer when at the age of twelve he played his first trumpet solo accompanied by the church pianist. While I played quite accurately in my key of B-flat, the pianist was accurate playing her notes in the key of C. We couldn't understand why the most horrible sounds were being heard. When I asked my trumpet teacher about my disaster, he simply said, "You didn't transpose—either of you!"

While scholars from the academic areas of theology, psychology, and the physical sciences may certainly reject this pseudo-Christianity described above, there is the need within the academic world to project sounds of hope that can be heard and accepted by and for a hurting humanity. While a solid interest in effectively integrating the various fields of study is frequently shown, the true value and sounds of each are made incomprehensible to the listener, who hears the different keys with no harmonious sound. Our world, as the world of yesterday, is calling for valid sounds of hope, a hope that will speak not only collectively but individually to the lonely, the hurting, and the disenfranchised who ask again and again, "Is there any hope for me?" Yes, there is for the "me" that seems lost in the world of multitudinous sounds, but who cannot tune in to a relevant "sound" that makes life worth living and in harmony.

Dr. Clinebell's insightful article, "Religion Can Make You Sick or Keep You Well," is relevant to our quest for hope. If true religion is one's ultimate concern, the concern is for the health of body, mind, and spirit.

Until those in need can hear sounds that speak living words of hope, however, illness and "dis-ease" will occur. An uneasy society is certainly in evidence until each of its components, the individuals, can hear and respond to sounds of hope, a hope that can only be found in its creator, the risen Christ!

The aforementioned "New Theology of Hope" is seemingly new in contemporary theological circles, but its real essence and dynamic found its greatest and real source in the Christ of hope, one who came to be that word, that answer for those who seemed hopeless. This risen Christ would and does project a sound that was transposed into a universal "key" that blends together the resources needed for body, mind, and spirit. Referenced earlier, the relevance of Orlo Strunk's call for balance would seem to validate our concern for a true integration, not competition. In essence, as Strunk has noted, it is not an option if we are to have a new a vision of psychology and, I would add, the vision of all true areas of theology, psychology, and the natural sciences.

It is a truism that human beings are incurably religious. To omit or deny one aspect or experience of religion in the life of an individual is to open that person to simply another belief or religion. In a world that is seeking meaning, the quest for something more, something beyond, is omnipresent. It is to this need that transposition must take place. The resources that are available and should be covered in real life are not to be seen as competitive but rather as complementary to our listening for new sounds of hope. Hope as our focal point can only be validated if and when its basis originates from all areas of study. Life is not an isolated occurrence, but an event that is from within and beyond time. Religion as ultimate concern must logically draw from multiple sources but its true sounds must be transposed into the right key.

As modern research is still in its infancy regarding the structure of reality, despite incomprehensible advances in physics and all of the natural sciences, it is admitting its infancy. We are assured that it is a quest that is always opening new avenues of truth. It is because of hope that human beings are clearly engaged in the process of finding life, its reality and its destiny. Completeness in research is never a possibility, but only a sense of being "in process" at least until the eschaton. Returning once more to the erudite mind of Moltmann, the end is really only a "new beginning."[3]

3. Moltmann, *In the End*, ix.

The concept of transposition, and thus the need to communicate and correlate within and among these varied areas of study, must also be found in the concept of "two worlds." Until a two-world concept of reality is recognized, the very basis of hope cannot be dealt with. Hope in itself is always present and yet beyond, but all too frequently we see both the fundamentalist mindset and that of the (so-called) liberal who do not accept this as valid. The fundamentalists focus their concern beyond this life and often disparage present living (except insofar as its profits and luxuries are available). The liberal-minded live only in the present or "one world is enough belief." The latter is just recently illustrated by Gordon Kaufman's concept of life as only an accidental event with no concept of a personal God, and when confronted by John Polkinghorne's review in *Theology Today*, Kaufman's pseudo-scientific view was negated by any critical reader.[4]

In my research on hope, as well as from decades of pastoral work both in the local parish and in the mental health clinic, this dual concept of reality was and is increasingly shown to be the "only answer." We cannot be in touch with reality if our focus is only on the "now." While this is true, neither can we healthfully focus only on the "other world" and negate our present. Once more the need to transpose one's thoughts in order to play in harmony is important in this two-world approach. If our world is to hear relevant and valid sounds of hope, the instruments of the present must be keyed in with those who would focus on the new world and/or the world beyond.

The glaring evidence of the lack of transposition is to be seen not only in a revival of the skepticism of the eighteenth and nineteenth centuries, but also in a new acceptance of a rabid fundamentalist couched in modern garb, yet playing the same old tunes in their "own key" of hate and violence. Can there be a resolution to this contrasting dilemma? Yes, for there are valid truths in each "camp." The fundamentalist is too often not transposing their concern for the beyond into the hurts and needs of today. And as noted before, the old liberal stance has refocused on this day only, negating the inner need of human beings for something more.

Anthony Reading offers a relevant answer to the problem when he quotes from the seventeenth-century scholar Francis Bacon, who said, "The greatest obstacle to the growth of understanding is that men [sic]

---

4. Polkinghorne, Review of "In the Beginning . . . Creativity."

despair and think things impossible."[5] Certainly only a valid hope can counteract the tones of despair as relevant today as in Bacon's era.[6]

Our concern regarding the need to recognize and actually live in two words is an imperative and, in fact, a reality for both the believer and the non-believer. But when one becomes cognizant of the "more" exploration of transposition, there are other worlds in the life of human beings. These different concepts cannot help but influence one's concept of the *Weltanschauung*. In a world of many sounds, the call for the sound of hope is muffled by competing sounds of despair. But despite these sounds, while certainly sending forth notes of confusion and hopelessness, there are distinctive other sounds of multiple worldviews. These too need to be transposed in our understanding. Orlo Strunk had successfully addressed these problems in a monograph several years ago entitled, "Religion as Deviant Reality: The Psychology Theology Dilemma." In this article, Dr. Strunk brings into focus the various reality systems encountered by therapists with clients. Drawing from the work of the early psychologist of religion, William James, Strunk sets forth the essential dynamics of each "subuniverse of reality" that James has identified. Now, as at the turn of the twentieth century, these multiple "universes" appear "live and well."

There are seven various worldviews, as follows:

First is the world of physical theory as we instinctively apprehend it, a world of sensory experiences of such qualities as heat, color, and sound along with such forces of life as chemical affinity, gravity, and electricity all existing on the surface of things.

Second is the subuniverse of the world of science primarily concerned with the laws of the universe.

Third is the world illustrated by logic, mathematics, ethics, and other forms of discipline.

Fourth is the world of "the idols of the trade," illusions or prejudices common to the race. For James, all educated people identify these prejudices as one subuniverse, but some modern social scientists have noticed the scientific truth of one period may become the idol of the trade of another.

Fifth is the world that James designated the "supernatural world," with

5. Reading, *Hope and Despair*, 173.
6. Strunk, "Religion as Deviant Reality."

its notes of heaven, hell, mythology, etc.

Sixth is the subuniverse of reality of individual opinions, which are numerous.

Seventh is listed as the world of sheer madness and vagary, which is also infinite.

As James noted, any one of these worlds can become real for us if it enters into our emotional active life.[7]

These worldviews of *Weltanschauung* are not only those that occur within the psychotherapeutic encounters. These varying world views are real and present in the various areas of study. Those who affirm a particular theological bent, along with earnest thinkers in the various scholastic disciplines of science, psychology, etc., are prime candidates for "transposition." Our concept, as affirmed in this chapter, is that to achieve an adequate symphony of hope, the participants must of necessity play in the same key. Only by accepting and seeing with an appreciation for the *Weltanschauung* of the other can this be achieved. Truth is universal and yet, as James so cogently identified at the beginning of *The Principles of Psychology*, there are subuniverses of comprehension, and these must be addressed if we are to really hear sounds of hope as they were originally written.

If we are to transpose the source of hope from the various wells of knowledge, we must seek valid truth from each. Let each play its own instrument of truth, but, as noted, in the same key. For too long our world has heard a cacophony of sound, much of which could be and are clearly written sounds of hope, but the "audience," our society, hears each in its own key. And we wonder why the world hears much discord in the "off-key" renditions of what is said to be reality! Real hope must be projected in a universal language, both in theory and in praxis. The accounts of pain and death that surrounded Bishop Tutu, Jürgen Moltmann, and Viktor Frankl, along with countless others, gave rise to exciting new truths. These new concepts of truth that we now experience in their writings were designed in, and by, the fires of experience. Here are sounds of hope that were heard even amidst intolerable pain and despair. We have their rich insight from which to draw our own hopes, but their experiences

---

7. Ibid.

give us, as perhaps as no others do, proof of the impact of both theory and praxis for an active hope.

We, as persons of today, can initiate our own thinking regarding hope's validity, but we owe a debt to such individuals who proclaimed and lived out hope when all else seemed to be "out of tune" with life. It is individuals like those mentioned who give to us a prime example of transposition. The symphony of hope, in essence, must come from one's own existential experiences, and the power of the future can and must begin in the "now" of our lives. The "now" of our lives must not be limited to our present nor only to an imminent God. Why? Despite the reality of the need for a sense of presence, the mystery, the sense of one alone and beyond is of ultimate importance.

If hope is focused only in the narrow concept of human rationalization, its future would always be limited to finite proportions. To see and comprehend all mystery is not possible, for that would seem to negate mystery itself. If we, as seekers of truth, attempt to relegate all senses of the transcendent to our finite level, by this very move we would be contradicting the search for two worlds, assured that all is now known. How relevant is Alistair McGrath's book entitled *The Unknown God*, when McGrath's whole theme is a portrayal of a God who is so very near and yet is the incomprehensible unknown.[8] As modern science is becoming increasingly aware, the whole is not confined to, nor explored fully, in the laboratory, nor is it explainable. Our need is to follow hope as it stimulates and opens new doors of knowledge, expanding our vision, ever drawing us beyond the "now." As we become more aware of our "now," it too will be a step toward a new beginning, a beginning beyond what once was seen as a closed system.

Our transposition of hope can be that new beginning of hearing and responding to the hope being drawn from the future, the future of God. Only as we begin to write a new score, a new symphony of hope, can this world, this part of the universe, begin to find its place and its role in a symphony of peace, hope, and life. Certainly with all of its discord (which will be dealt with later in this work), this world with all of its once harmonious existence, anxiously awaits to hear these sounds. It is exciting to hear hints of harmony as the various areas of thought are recognizing

8. *Unknown God*, 1.

the need for transposition of ideas different in essence, but all of which are needed to build a true symphony of hope.

One of the most innovative and incisive sojourns for this hope for correlation between the sciences and metaphysics is occurring at the Center for Theological Inquiry in Princeton, New Jersey. The dream, the brainchild of the fourth president of Princeton, Dr. James McCord, has already made its mark. Illustrative of this is its recent four-year symposium on science and eschaton already mentioned in this work. At that conference, my call for a transposition was already occurring (and without my direction!). Drawing from some of the world's premier scientists, philosophers, and theologians, the very creative group has dared to cross into and listen to sounds of hope from other performers, thus building of a symphony of hope. Here the true concept of transposition is and continues to be exercised. The language of hope that is being written by such open-minded scholars is able to initiate hope in a world that is so frequently bereft of hope. From terrorism to a haunting fear that all will sooner or later become engulfed in nothingness, modern humans live in fear, fear of the "now" and of a future that seems to project hopelessness.

This need, this sense of fear, and a desperate call for help, was cogently illustrated by a small boy. When asked what he wanted to be when he grew up, he simply said, "I just want to grow up."[9] How very relevant regarding all scholarly attempts to make sense of life via science, philosophy, or theology. If there is no future nor assured destiny, all is in vain. Only by an adequate eschatological focus can this need be answered. Returning to Polkinghorne as he writes concerning this aspect of reality, "Not only our individual life but also the universe is doomed to physical decay. This scientific insight of the twentieth century does pose a great threat to theology and the faith of all religion; i.e., if it is all heading toward an abyss of nothing, why bother?"[10] It is such disturbing facts as these that give fuel to the proponents of despair, both the radical prophets of doom and those in the political and secular arena as well. Hope is seen as an element with no permanence or destiny, our once solid theological concepts are just "concepts." If, however, our vision goes beyond the finite, the human reach, there is, as Moltmann would affirm, "another way."

9. Polkinghorne, *Science and Providence*, 3.
10. Polkinghorne and Welker, eds., *End of the World*, 7.

This way is incarnate in the risen Christ who affirms, "Behold, I make all things new!"

The discordant sound of a purely rational stance based on human limitation is certainly a factor to be faced by all religions. Yet it is this writer's contention that there can be, and is, a logical transposition of the hard facts of scientific calculations with an honest theological view. Reality is not encased in only that which can be measured with human instruments. This fact is becoming increasingly accepted even by the most advanced thinkers in the scientific area. Thus it is at this point of our study that a solid eschatology must be envisioned by those in both the fields of laboratory science and those within the realm of metaphysics. In essence, all of us are engaged in a dialogue with destiny. A world so often shaken not only by its tragic wounds, but also by its very advancement in science, awaits some sounds of hope and security. How relevant, even today, are the words of Franklin Roosevelt in his inaugural speech in 1932 when he said, "We have a rendezvous with destiny."[11] The challenge today, in the twenty-first century, is to determine and tune ourselves to a hope that will encounter this rendezvous with strength and clear insight. The key to any real transposition is for each instrument to tune its truth, its concept, into a related dynamic. A true and open-ended theory is one that allows for new vistas regarding God and God's purpose in an eschatological stance. Likewise, a true scientist must, by the very definition, be ever in quest of the new, being aware (as should the theologian and psychologist) that the new might be from another colleague and seeker of truth. A song of years ago would seem to give us a fresh view of reality. The song is entitled "Love is a Many Splendored Thing," and certainly reality is a "many splendored thing." There is beauty in living in the reality of simply "being."

Hans Weder, also a member of the four-year study group at The Center for Theological Inquiry held at Princeton, links a valuable contribution to our quest for an adequate transposition by noting that:

> The dialogue between theology and natural science can only make sense if they share a common subject. My suggestion is to define reality as this subject. This implies however a certain epistemological disposition in both: theology and natural science both producing a construction of reality that can and must be distinguishable from reality itself . . . different sciences can be taken as

11. Excerpt from FDR's inaugural address.

multidimensional approaches to the same reality and dialogue
aims to broaden the notion of the real by taking into account as
many dimensions as possible.[12]

From this erudite notation by Weder, the vital necessity of dialogue
is strength, and the need for a valid transposition of language becomes
even more relevant. For as Weder has suggested, our subject is and should
be reality. As we have seen, reality is not an isolated element or study but
encompasses every possible source of knowledge from which to envision
its composition. Certainly a composition is not one single approach, but
that which draws from however many sources are relevant.

All too frequently what is projected as "reality" is only a pessimistic
view of life here and beyond. Yet nothing could be further from the truth.
In essence, if we see reality as that which is multifaceted, one must return
again to the one who was and is the creator. The creator never did, and
never could, by its very being, create despair and hopelessness. A world
that seems to thrive on these elements finds little solace in the fundamentalist or dispensationalist theology, nor in the extreme left, neither of
which has dealt with primary sources such as Holy Scripture. Meanwhile
the world continues to listen and wait for a clear transposition of what
this writer would label correlated truth or facts. Yet at times it appears that
those who listen and wait for true sounds of hope continue to hear only
isolated enactments that neither correlate nor send forth clear sounds of
hope and truth. To listen and/or watch much of what passes for entertainment is a depiction of loneliness and a pattern of life and all of the violence needed to hold one's attention. Speaking as one who has been on the
cutting edge of reality in the local church and in psychological endeavors,
as well as in part-time college teaching, the eschatological note was and is
ever present. Modern human beings are either overtly or implicitly ever
aware of a "beyond." While these overt appearances or verbalizations may
not seem obvious, the apprehension is still there. Could it possibly be that
when individuals find themselves entertained by TV violence, they are
in essence trying to see violence as "just an act?" With various scenes of
death, could this be another escape that death for oneself is only an act
with an expected ending of a drama?

The oft-quoted question "What is life?" is in reality one frequented
with a solid eschatological note. While the fear of hell and the vengeance

12. Weder, "Metaphysics and Reality," 29.

of God experienced in another generation are no longer articulated, there does remain a haunting fear, as Tillich would say, "of non-being." On the other hand, human beings also fear life! What a dilemma! To such a situation, Clinebell is once again the epitome of relevance. He notes that inherent in human concern is a spiritual longing that must be satisfied. Reality, as we have continuously portrayed it, is more than a three-dimensional reality for Clinebell. The haunting fear we have can only be vanquished by a fresh belief that our universe is a friendly place. To meet the need of the emptiness of modern human beings is the dynamic opportunity and call for pastoral care. Clinebell apologetically indicts much of what passes for religion as that which pours spiritual gasoline on the widespread fires of violence, despair, meaninglessness, and injustice that are destroying the good life for millions of God's children in all cultures around our planet.[13]

The cries of God's children are seldom heard by the Christians on the "right." Presidents' prayer breakfasts are held at least annually and despite a "religious Christian stance," one must wonder if the participants hear the cries of those described by Clinebell. At this point, it must be noted that the situation is more than sincere individuals playing their sound in a wrong key, but more like entire groups playing with the wrong instrument! Instead of instruments of love, forgiveness, and passion for justice, their "instruments" are those of a coldness of heart, a passion for hate, violence, and enacting a self-appointed pseudo-messianic role.

The perpetual but hidden sense of cosmic loneliness is not a new feeling.[14] But in our incredible technological society its impact is more pervasive. Human beings feel that they are subjected to both outer and inner forces beyond their control. Again and again the so-called "modern human being" calls for help, for love, but these calls are only an echo in the hollow halls of existence. To these needs, a true theology of hope must speak in a language transposed into not only clear theory but addressing the concrete needs of every individual, friend and foe alike. Karl Barth's thoughts about addressing the needs of all persons regardless of creed were brought forth by a contemporary author, Michael Welker. Barth, while certainly holding the position as premier theologian of the twentieth century, was deeply aware of the need for a gospel to all peoples. As Welker notes, Barth was certain that Jesus Christ died for the Marxist,

13. Clinebell, "Religion Can Make You Sick or Keep You Well," 2.

14. Ibid.

the captor, and the fascist; i.e., the gospel of Jesus Christ was for all, not a select few.[15] While many of his time and ours would disagree covertly, if not overtly, regarding a gospel for all, such was not the case with Barth. In reality, Barth could be listed as an earlier promoter of hope, even before the advent of Moltmann, Pannenberg, and others. In essence, hope is that which is to be offered to all people, both individually and collectively. This is a hopeful sign! Too often individuals who carry the name of "Christian" have either visible or invisible "boundaries" as to when, who, and how the gospel should reach. This writer, after revisiting Barth's writings, affirms that both the earlier and later Barth had invaluable truth to share regarding hope. Attacked by both sides of the theological spectrum, Barth continued to exude a profound cognizance of hope for all. When asked if he was a universalist, Barth candidly answered, "I won't say I am, and I won't say I'm not." What transposition that only Barth could affirm!

15. Polkinghorne and Welker, eds., *End of the World.*

Chapter 5

Sounds of Hope:
Composing a Symphony

IN A WORLD OF discord, sounds of hope would seem to be almost impossible. Yet, philosophically speaking, we must recognize the incontrovertible fact that if a problem exists there must be an answer, however distant or difficult it is. A psychology of hope and its theological counterpart focuses not only on theory but also on practice. Its language and sound must be played in the same key if real harmony and its true intended sound are to be heard.

Throughout this work, we have focused on a projection of sources of truth from not only theology and psychology, but from the physical sciences as well. As has been unwavering in evidence, eschatology is that which permeates all of life. In fact, if there is no concept of a purposeful eschatology, all of our explorations, explanatory correlations from theory to concrete reality would be an exercise in futility. If all of what we envision as life, meaning, etc., were only destined for "nothingness," why even wrestle with thoughts, however profound? In fact, if this picture of gloom and destruction were all that awaits us, the nihilists would be correct: "all is nothing, nothing is all."

Happily such is not the basis of reality. The cosmos is designed in a friendly motif. There is a focus of life not only collectively but also individually. The person, the one made in God's image (who is often effaced), is still a dynamic focal point in this beautiful universe. It remains to be seen what real hope will produce. From the anecdote mentioned in the prelude to further studies regarding hope, the basis of life is hope—an actual hope which initiates another way out of the depths of darkness and despair and the tendency to simply give up.

In a world of discord, this would seem to be almost impossible. Yet philosophically we must recognize that the very fact a problem exists demands a possible answer. Thus only a true sense of hope can begin to break the barrier of discord in life's symphony.

A psychology of hope and its theological counterpart must focus not only on theory but also on praxis. Its language and sound must be played in the same key if real harmony is to be heard. While our world appears to be deaf regarding hope for tomorrow let alone today, in the inner being of the self can be "heard" a call for hope. "Is anybody listening?" is what is spoken in the silent language of the heart. Speaking to this need is our focus as we must deal with not only our present but also our conceptual aspect of eschatology. We are not merely a purposeless collection of atoms existing for a few or more years in an unfeeling universe.

The fact of human beings and their relationship to a creator is being accepted not only by theology, psychology, and philosophy, but very recently by those in the world of physical science. In fact there is research being initiated that seems to focus on the fact that we are "wired for God." What a variation from the older concept of the so-called modernist, who in earlier years dismisses the human being as just searching for answers. If we begin to accept the new reality that we are in a sense "more than before" and in reality "citizens of two worlds," a sound of harmony can begin to be heard. Our now, our present, will be seen as part of the eschatological plan when this occurs. In our quest for a total "score" in the real life performances of which we are a part, there can be a symphony of hope if and when each instrument will utilize and continue this specific sound of hope. There can and will be a harmonious sound: the sound of a new kingdom, the kingdom of God so articulately portrayed in the world of Moltmann and others.

In a world so filled with hopelessness—hopelessness generated not only by the secular sector, but also by those in the so-called religious sector—it is no surprise that these individuals play only in a minor key. A world waiting for a sound of hope in a major key continues to hear the sounds emitted by a secular society. Once more we can see and hear the sounds of emptiness and the hollow echoes of hurting beings in caverns of everyday life.

But the good news is that the creator God and his Son the risen Christ do hear these sounds of despair! Yet, in one sense, God's hearing of the sound is not enough. Only action by an actively hopeful society can be the answer. The incarnate Christ did come into the depths of human despair and by his death and resurrection open up the gate of despair and death. Each of us are now called to be agents of hope by leading those in need into the light "beyond the cave" of darkness. (Remember Plato's cave illustration?)

A definitive change has been initiated in the psychological community. Whereas the emphasis in psychology as well as in the medical sciences was to focus on problems of human beings, such is no longer the only or chief focus. In place of studies focusing on the negative aspects of human psychology and the physical body, the new emphasis is on the positive, the hopeful dynamics of a person. Essentially we are moving from an emphasis on depth psychology (a needed focus of change, as well) to a "height psychology." Indicators of the change occurred in a recent college class this writer was teaching. In an introductory course in psychology, it was not surprising to hear erroneous conceptions of what psychology really is. When the question was raised regarding the purpose of psychology, the first answer was, "To find what is wrong with us!" Upon learning that our focus was to be not only the negative but also the positive, a different tone emerged in the class.

To hear such response from an introductory class in psychology was not surprising, but the more devastating truth is to see and hear too many individuals both in the fields of science and psychology and also religion who focus on the despair of life. And the latter are supposed to be, as noted, "purveyors of hope!" Once more the poignant question must be answered, "Where has hope gone?" Could it be that its essence and dynamic have been either lost or submerged in sounds of despair, a despair generated by fundamental sounds of hate and vengeance (except for the chosen few)? While the gloom of the fundamentalist camp is all too obvious, so too are the sounds of hopelessness, not only from secular poets and writers, but also from those who attempt to be authorities in religion.

The need for more sounds of hope is not a question to be debated. Yet those who should be in the forefront of this challenge are all too frequently promoting sounds in their own key with minimal sounds of hope. However, there have been and continue to be scholars in both the scientific and medical fields, as well as psychologists and theologians, who affirm and prove the power of hope. Bernie Siegel, Carl Simonton, the late Norman Cousins, along with psychiatrist Karl Menninger, are verifying the validity of hope not only as a metaphysical entity, but as a solid concrete element. Hope does work. Hope does make a difference—often between life and death.

Nevertheless, however much the human society of which we are a part advances in science, medicine, and psychology, all is once more seen as an exercise in futility if this is all. Unless, and until, an adequate concept of eschatology and its role in the cosmic plan is envisioned, all is in vain. To look at the vast reaches of space on a starry night gives us a sense of both the glory of human beings and the feeling of being finite. Brian Greene in his closing statement in *The Fabric Of the Cosmos*, gives us at least a partial answer when he said that to look above us is to feel something of the dynamic of ourselves and the universe beyond, a sense of relationship to that which is above and beyond and yet within us.[1] The reverence of open-minded cosmologists such as Greene may be seen in his closing statements after discussing the deep physical laws of the universe. He states, "for me there would be nothing more poetic, no outcome more graceful, no unification more complete, than for us to confirm our theories of the ultrasmall—our theories about the ultramicroscopic make-up of space, time, and matter—by turning our most powerful telescopes skyward and gazing silently at the stars."[2] To gaze beyond is certainly an exercise in expanded theology, but to look at the impact is to also return to the finite, the microcosm of our own self, and being the "me" of existence.

It is to this "me" that a physician such as Jerome Groopman has focused in his book *The Anatomy of Hope*. In this author's groundbreaking treatise on the increasing literature on body and mind, the power of hope is articulately illustrated. In case after case, Dr. Groopman projected the interrelationships of one's hope and its impact on the healing process.

The dynamic power of hope is lucidly described in a clinical trial of real surgery versus sham surgery. In an individual with knee problems, arthroscopic surgery was given and justified for real need. Another patient participated in a placebo-type surgery. All of the set-ups of surgery were performed except the actual operation. As Groopman noted, the expected results of those having real surgery were successful, but the placebo participant had an equal benefit.[3]

1. Greene, *The Fabric of the Cosmos*, 493.
2. Ibid.
3. Groopman, *The Anatomy of Hope*, 174.

The only empirical explanation was that belief and expectation likely release powerful endorphins and enkophy from the pseudo surgery. Is this only an anecdote (a once-only occurrence) or could the dynamics of hope be in control rather than an invasive action in the life of human beings?

To explore the dynamics of hope and to write a symphony of hope has been and continues to be a passion with this writer. As one who has completed over forty-seven years in pastoral ministry, more than thirty years as a psychotherapist in both private and public clinics along with more than twenty years as a part-time college teacher, the dynamics of hope have been a constant element in these roles. The result and essence of hope has been and continues to be explored in both theory and praxis. How often have I seen downcast clients come to our clinic or my office and leave with a new outlook because of the element of hope being affirmed and integrated into their lives. Hope is a defining and transforming element in the lives of individuals and society collectively.

The late Paul Johnson, one of pastoral psychology's pioneers, was very person-centered. Yet he was equally concerned with the community in which one lives. His classic affirmation was (to paraphrase), "We are interpersonal people."[4] In essence, we are made for interpersonal activity. While we must not negate the dynamic individualism of a person, nevertheless we need each other. Hope, then, is not only an effective element in the lives of individuals but of society collectively. A hopeful spirit that permeates a group, whether in business or church groups, is certainly an element that often determines the group's success or failure. While it is a medical fact that a change in mindset can alter neurons chemically, both in a laboratory setting and in the clinic one might ask if this could be true in a collective setting. Could individuals in "combination" exert multiple changes in a group dynamic effort? One can only wonder and ask, "what if?" Returning to Paul Johnson's theory of interpersonal psychology, which is still relevant today, he has noted, "It is my conviction that interacting persons are the field of psychology—nothing less than personality is an adequate functioning unit for psychology."[5]

Our society, which in the not too distant past had relegated eschatology to an irrelevant memory, has experienced a radical change.

4. Johnson, *Psychology of Religion*, 8.
5. Ibid.

Widespread apprehension about life as we have known it has been present since the threat of nuclear war appeared on the horizon. But while the horror of a possible nuclear war has overshadowed our world since the advent of the bomb, even this threat is now being ignored to a degree. Why? With the threat of a terrorist attack from within, as well as beyond, our shores, society and individuals now seek a strength from a higher power. The fear of nonbeing, however negative on the surface, is still churning within. Yet in a strange paradox of this fear of dying, there is the fear of life itself that drives more people to suicide than die as a result of homicide.

Moltmann's work in this area, especially *In the End—the Beginning: The Life of Hope*, is once again relevant.[6] The projection of seeing beyond the present chaos, the ever-deepening despair is made possible only by accepting the hope for a new beginning. The God of the past and present is also the God of the future and his kingdom is coming.

Referring to fears both past and present, Moltmann states regarding apocalyptic fear, "The biblical apocalypses are not pessimistic scenarios of a global catastrophe which merely disseminate fear and terror so that human beings are paralysed by the corresponding belief in their doom. These apocalypses are messages of hope in danger, an encouragement to see the danger and to clearly resist it. They keep alive hope in the faithfulness of God."[7] And while Moltmann cautions against being blind to fear and catastrophe, he also affirms the fact that these scenarios must be seen "as if we 'look through the horizon,' as the Indonesian word for hope puts it. 'He who endures to the end will be saved.'"[8] While radical prophets of doom predict annihilation, our God of hope assures his creatures that he is still in control.

Our quest for valid sounds of hope find its answer in a multiplicity of persons, places, and creation as a whole. It is from these sources that our symphony of hope is being brought to at least a preliminary performance and/or "practice session." All too often, though, we seem to hear only the discordant source of various instruments as each sounds its own note. Yet when the conductor rises and lifts his baton, suddenly there is a sense and sound of togetherness as each plays its own role. To initiate a picture and

6. Moltmann, 51–53.

7. Ibid., 51.

8. Ibid.

sound of a hope symphony is our total concern. It is our all-encompassing plan to draw our sound of hope not from isolated areas of study, however valid in their own right, but from real contributing projects from not only the humanities, e.g., psychology, philosophy, and religion, but from the physical and biological sciences as well. Only if a panoramic picture is initiated regarding a true symphony of hope, each area of study must then insert its aspect of reality into a blending of all truth that relates to a total sound of hope.

In a world that is seemingly progressing toward destruction either in natural disaster or the wars of humanity, its inhabitants seek answers.[9] Their answers have been found in such diverse sources as Jung's animistic culture to our "modern" culture of the Left Behind series with predictions of doom for all but the "chosen few." But this is not all. While we can more easily dismiss the narrow archaic pattern of the fundamentalist dispensationalists et al., the so-called experts on biblical theology are equally as closed in their theological thinking. This group of what one could label as pseudo-biblical authorities, e.g., the Jesus Seminar, and their self-title of "major theologians," assert that anything beyond concrete experience cannot be. Once more the closed thinking on both sides of the theological spectrum is a barrier to our quest for harmony and search for a symphony of hope.

While such closed approaches to the road to hope are so blatantly in evidence, the sword of Damocles seems so very near.

Amidst these sounds of despair, death, and meaninglessness, can there be true sounds of hope? Can there be an answer that does not negate the intellect of science with its monumental advances, nor negate or ignore the dynamics and basis of faith in the resurrection? All too often the barrier to a true sound of hope is that each "instrument" plays its own tune or key and either negates or ignores the score, scarcely glancing at the master conductor! Could there really be one who is in control, or is our world, our very being, simply an unimportant event in a lonely, meaningless universe? If there is one conductor who knows every note and every instrument along with knowledge of the players, then the very fact of existence would make sense. The sound of discord that seems to fill the world of today as in yesterday could and would be transformed into a symphony of hope.

9. Polkinghorne and Welker, eds., *End of the World*, 1.

In a monograph by Orlo Strunk Jr., the need for a worldview of psychology is poignantly set forth. The need is evidenced for a solid eschatological note in life itself, and especially in the area of psychology. Drawing upon such thinkers as the late Gordon Allport, Milton Rokeach, and Adrian van Kaam, Strunk affirms the need for a worldview, a *Weltanschauung*.[10] As Strunk succinctly notes, too often even so-called religion-based therapists or pastoral counselors have avoided or ignored the value and dynamics of exploring or using solid theology to answer the ever present question of existence itself. To quote Strunk once more relative to this, he affirms that fact that, "It is one thing to accept at a theological level the world view factor as a legitimate subject for the psychological profession. It is another thing to deal creatively within the process of psychology."[11]

As Strunk further affirmed and observed regarding this need, it is certainly a fact that those in the religious therapy area should be able to accept and draw from sources beyond the present. This might not be only in theory but in actual practice. On a personal note, with this writer, having been in both the theological field and that of pastoral counseling, the eschatological note is one that is always sounded, whether overtly or implicitly, in therapeutic encounters. The quest for life and the hope that can give meaning can never be successful if one focuses on the present. A present, however meaningful, calls for a future. To successfully fulfill one's individual role in a symphony of hope, the eschatological note must be present, or the true sound of hope will only echo in a chasm of emptiness and despair!

Further Sounds of Healing Eschatology

In a hurting world, any sound of hope is listened to, but all too frequently its true sounds are muffled or distorted by conflicting sounds. In a world full of multiple sounds, some of which are so very disheartening, it is difficult to discern the valid sounds of true hope. Announcements of violence and despair are composed not only by those seemingly beyond the religious spectrum, as noted, but by those who proclaim their own version of hope via advertising the right way and the right product for happiness.

10. Strunk, "The World View Factor," 193.

11. Ibid., 199.

Our society is deluged with false hopes for a better world through accepting "offerings" of self-hope. Nevertheless, despite these erroneous routes to hope, the fact is increasingly affirmed by contemporary psychology and theology that a vital religious experience and code is an immeasurable healing event. As Robert Emmons stated, "Optimal psychological health and well being occur when different elements of personality are integrated into a more or less coherent whole. Spirituality in its essential nature is concerned with personal transformation—personal transformation may be a surer road to wholeness than other strategies that have been attempted and that have failed."[12]

Spirituality, along with its ultimate goal and an adequate eschatological view and its realization, must be seen as that which gives real hope. Real hope must be based not only on the concrete, the present, but on the reality of spirit. But the real self is that for which only an eschatological view can suffice. The world with its ever increasing confusion, despite incomprehensible advances in science, is still pierced by fear of life, of the unknown, and the very "why" of existence. The "more" of life is a perpetual element in the real thinking of human beings whenever one asks, "Why?"

It is to this need that one must go beyond the now, beyond that which can be experienced in the laboratory, however sophisticated, to find reality—a reality for life here and beyond. In Alistair McGrath's recent treatise on heaven, he presented C. S. Lewis' incisive definition of a certain belief in heaven. Lewis was aware of certain human emotion that points to a dimension of our existence beyond time and space. There is, as Lewis suggests, a "deep and intense feeling of longing within human beings, which no earthly object can experience or establish."[13]

To read Lewis is to see and hear one who has not accepted a simplistic theology of a beyond. He has wrestled with his own agnostic and atheistic views on the way to a belief in the transcendent. McGrath, one of England's younger scholars (but a prolific and noted one), is not intimidated by those who might scoff at his affirmation of hope, a hope grounded in the resurrection of Jesus Christ. For McGrath, Jesus is the ground of hope and gives that hope to all those who may suffer and die,[14]

12. Emmons, *The Psychology of Ultimate Concerns*, 136.

13. Quoted in McGrath, *Brief History of Heaven*, 133.

14. Ibid., 164.

which is certainly all of us. Despite a culture of skepticism on one side and a naïve theology of "last things" on the other, one must then logically seek an encompassing psychology and theology that does answer the vital questions of everyone, "Is there any hope? And is there something or someone beyond?" Hurting persons from every strata of life are listening for a sound of hope, hope for their existential need and the fulfillment of the self in pilgrimage.

The philosopher Alfred N. Whitehead in his work entitled, *Science and the Modern World* (yes, modern, even though published in 1947), affirms that mind and organization were the ultimate reality; i.e., reality is how we organize and conceive of what we know as objective or concrete. Would not this theory seem to validate our premise that spirituality—more than the purely physical—is the core of reality? Quoting Ornstel and Erlist, Anthony Reading gives credibility to those thoughts as he states, "The world that made us is different from the world we have made."[15] Could it be that with all of our marginal achievements in a place called "planet earth," we have organized ourselves out of reality by closing off any sense of something or someone beyond us?

To read not only religious writings of both the left and the right, but to listen to physicists is to stimulate within us the definitive need to hear at least some "hint" of harmony in our very discordant society. The audience, those who would listen, does not need professional training to hear those oft noted discordant sounds. These attendees in the symphonic halls of life continue to hope for sounds of hope. Too often they have nothing to hear but continued sounds of despair, not only by those who claim no special religious longing but by those who affirm hope for only a "chosen few." As set forth in the chapter on transposition and its importance, again and again performers who know their instruments well continue to play in their own key listening to their own sound "while the band played on," as the old song cognizably notes! Meanwhile, in places such as Iraq, even as I write these chapters, sounds of hope are being drowned out by the sounds of gunfire and bombs provided by pseudo-biblical-believing Christians who have relied on building a new world via destruction of a wounded land. Olga Yaqob tells of searching for hope amidst the terror in Iraq during the Iran-Iraq War, the first Gulf War, and now the second. She vividly notes, "For twenty-four years of my life, since my first experience

15. Reading. *Hope and Despair*, 90-91.

of war in Iraq, I have lived the daily cross with and for my people. But, in faith, I have seen, beyond my daily cross, the brightness of the sun of God's hope in my life and in the lives of others. The face of God that I have seen through suffering makes me anticipate, with a hopeful heart, what: 'eye hath not seen, nor ear heard, [what has not] entered into the heart of man, the things which God hath prepared for them that love him' (1 Cor 2:9, KJV)."[16]

For those such as this individual, permeated with the effects of war, to hear her solid affirmation of hope validated is to see and hear hope in praxis. This was hope written beyond the scholar's textbook, but on the element of real life however painful. A true symphony of hope can and must be heard in situations such as this and countless others.

16. Yaqob, "The Face of God," 15–16.

Chapter 6

Sounds of Hope:
a Symphony of Hope in Praxis

IN THE WORLD OF music, the symphony is, in essence, multiple instruments being played by individuals who strive for a unified sound with a blending of individual sounds. The sounds of the blending are more than the sound of each individual when played in a solo role. While there are places in the musical score for solo performances, the real symphonic sound is the utilization of all instruments led by the master conductor.

In composing a symphony of hope, it is that same pattern of blending, the result of individual sounds, which will build that new sound. The reality of life and its destiny can only be seen and heard when each participant begins to contribute his or her own specialty into a holistic sound—the sound of hope. As a world existing in a state so bereft of hope strives to hear some hint of hope, these sounds can come only when all of the instruments of reality are beginning to play in union. Life is more than that which is on the surface of experience.

In Ben Campbell Johnson's book *Living Before God*, we have a superb affirmation of the need to see and hear more than that which we may comprehend on the surface of life. "When we renounce the flat world of sight and sense as the whole of reality, a new world of enchantment and mystery begins to be born. It is not that the material world is unreal but it is incomplete. Neither is the enchanted world of spirit new; rather we are recharging our organs of perception . . . the heart and ears of the soul to notice what has been there all along. Perhaps our culture is finally waking up after centuries of sleep."[1]

Our world is not complete in only one dimension, and the reality that is sought can only be grasped if and when its inhabitants accept the

1. Johnson, *Living Before God*, 69.

49

fact of a dimension beyond the now of our lives. To affirm the need for an adequate eschatological sound in building a symphony of hope is an imperative if the really real is to be experienced.

For over four decades, this writer has listened to sounds of despair emanating from both the parish and the clinic. The unmet need has been and continues to be an awareness that there is hope. Yes, hope available for the lonely, the hurting, the one living in a state of meaninglessness and feeling that there are no real sounds of hope and harmony in a discordant world. In the words of my former teacher, the late John Dixon Copp, "The more we listen beneath the surface, the closer we come to reality."[2]

If we focus on the almost perpetual scene of violence and death on our TV screens, our picture of life will appear as a world out of control. A darkened world is searching for a light in this dilemma, a dilemma that only a vital light of hope can disperse. A one-dimensional view can never initiate this needed hope. Only when we look beyond the now of life and see with eyes of faith, of image, of hope, and listen to new sounds emanating from the source of hope, the risen Christ, can a symphony of hope be composed.

In any symphonic composition there are multiple notes for a complete score. Each instrumentalist is to play his or her own special part and sound, thereby contributing to the beauty of combined instruments. To have a symphony is to have a theme, a title portrayed, the picture and source of hope. Hope is not a new innovation or discovery by even our most revered theologians of hope nor by their psychological counterparts and philosophers.

Nevertheless the revolutionary dynamics of hope finds their source from the risen Christ, who brought hope from despair and life from death. To hope is not to escape from reality but is that which, in essence, initiates all achievement in even our highly technological world. Hope in its most basic definition is always a "not yet" and unchanging element. For whether one accepts any concept of "belief" at all, every person lives by hope. Real hope is never an idle wish, or wishful thinking, but that which sees and hears beyond the finite, the "now" of the present.

From the earnest homemaker who hopes her meal will turn out satisfactorily to the space scientist at Cape Canaveral, each hopes for success. Thus, to live beyond mere existence is to hope for something more,

2. John Dixon Copp, Boston University School of Theology, lecture in "Psychology of Mysticism," 1953.

a more than seeing through the myopic lens of life and hearing only the sounds of silence, a silence echoing in corridors of hopelessness.

Hope, whether envisioned as a verb or a noun, is not, then, a new invention by either the theologian or psychologist of hope. It is that something more: the other way which opens a closed world to that which is really new. This new symphony of hope can only be achieved if and when each participant from the various areas of learning participates in a "key" that gives a harmonious sound in this discordant world.

Theology and psychology are always in a state of flux, as is cosmology, which hopes to pierce at least some of the secrets of space. To be alive is to be able to produce and reproduce and do so with hope. The statement that we are in a state of change and/or transition is as old as creation itself. While our technologies are perpetually making every new creation or achievement out of date, this has always been the situation. Only the rapidity, the unbelievable speed of change, is really different.

Indications of these changes are to be seen in the changing panorama in the giants of theology, psychology, and science. Even the new theology of hope is no longer new, and modernity is no longer modern. The universe of which we are a part is still in transition. The Tillichs and Ferres have given way to the new theologians of hope, a la Moltmann and Pannenberg, who are dominating contemporary theology. In the field of science, and especially the area of cosmology, Einstein and others, while still revered for their contributions, are replaced by cosmologists such as Brian Greene and Trinh Xuan Thuan.

While we see and hear of the old passing, there is the fact that there will always be the new, the hoped for, upon which we can focus. Dreams of yesterday can and will become the reality of the present as the future breaks in to our "now." Pop psychology, e.g., the Primal Scream, new theologies that do not create, and outdated cosmologies are buried in the reduced section of contemporary bookstores.

While many changes have occurred and continue with undiminished rapidity, the questions must be asked, "What is stable if there is such a thing as reality, and what is really 'real' or new? Is there any possibility that there is an answer to this world so out of tune?" Amidst these sounds of death and despair, the call is sounded either overtly or implicitly for hope. Yes, hope that there can be a symphony of hope that can be played to a world that has waited so long and seemingly in vain.

The answer to this need is being formulated not only by the theologians of hope, the psychologists and philosophers of hope, by those who are within the halls and laboratories of scientific research. Now even the cosmologists are taking a new and visionary look at not only the fear of a fragile universe, but the possibility of a new concert of reality, where the spirit is once more paramount in importance.

The previously marginalized concern of spirit is now "in." Spirit and its dynamics are looked at as the key to reality. It is no longer true that only the ideas that are visible and concrete can be accepted.

From the sophisticated laboratories of science to the inquiring university students of today, the quest is for more of the unseen and the mystical. As Bernie Siegel spoke regarding his approach to medicine, by explaining the unconditional love of self and others is a strong factor in healing.[3] To look at the human being from a physical standpoint is to see more than that which is composed of the chemical content. This miracle of creation is more than meets not only the physical eye, but the laboratory picture as well. The organization of what was once looked upon as only physical in one sense, is a microcosm of reality and microcosm beyond.

To be a person is to be part of the spiritual reality of life. Langdon Gilkey, while not being categorized as a theologian of hope, nevertheless offers a sound affirmation of the need to accept this word of sovereignty over life—the word of hope, coming from the author of hope, God and creator and risen Lord. Quoting the biblical proclamation of God's word, Marty notes, "I am the LORD, and there is no other. I formed the light and created darkness. I make peace and create disaster. I the LORD do all these things."[4] At one's first reading of Gilkey, one is hard-pressed to feel a sense of hope until we read beneath the surface. If we see and feel his affirmation of God's sovereignty, the fact of hope as the ultimate resource to affect change in both culture and persons, then Gilkey's note has a vital note to add to a symphony of hope. If we can really affirm the fact that hope is a reality and not a wistful possibility, then the need for God's sovereignty is very much in evidence. A theology and psychology of hope do not function as soloists in a true symphony of hope. Each one plays its own unique sound amidst the cacophony of despair and confusion so easily heard.

3. Siegel, *Peace, Love and Healing*.
4. Marty, "Let Us Now Praise Langdon Brown Gilkey, 1919–2004," 92.

One of my favorite pastimes (and present activities) is to browse in a mega bookstore like Barnes and Noble or Borders. After purchasing a gourmet coffee (to at least ease my conscience regarding the fact that I read more than I buy), I proceed to search for interesting works in my own areas of interest. As I peruse the areas of non-fiction, both secular and religious, an almost perpetual theme is in evidence. The population of today, at almost every level, is concerned with the future and what it may or may not bring. Politicians of both major parties, along with the lesser known, are projecting multiple concepts on how to fix our world.

Meanwhile at the religious section, I am quickly introduced to the end-of-the-world literature of the oft-read prophets of doom. If I linger a while longer, I see spiritual writers who are lay persons with no academic background filling the shelf space. Meanwhile I ask myself the question, "Why do people seem to reach for the superficial or the sensational in place of the solid writings also available?" Is it because individuals are seeking harmony in their lives? Could it be that the religious connotation of faith has failed to offer valid answers to a world so out of tune? And the search goes on.

It is to individuals of all walks of life that our projected symphony of hope is focused. Our world is still the world to which the God of the universe sent his Son to be the ultimate hope. Despite many detours and obstacles of every kind, there can be a new road of hope, a hope that will initiate a new sound, a sound of a symphony of all participants who follow the master conductor.

Now I am deeply aware that in the postmodern world, where truth is to be conceived only by its relevance to each person and society, any concept of a unified sound may sound archaic and out of tune. Nevertheless, our focus in building this symphony of hope is not one of isolation but cooperation.

Our concern is to set forth a symphony of hope that will draw from all related areas of reality, from the microcosmic to the cosmic. An audacious endeavor? Not really. For if we are to set forth real hope, it must not only draw from the richest concepts of the inner person and society, but have a basis in a solid cosmology. As previously noted, all of our intellectual and social explorations will be an exercise in futility if there is no universe in which to live.

As the exciting treatise *The End of the World and the Ends of God* so brilliantly claims, there is a vital difference between human ends and the ends that are set forth by our creator. As one who has listened to innumerable sounds of theology and psychology, I have become increasingly cognizant of a need for a correlation of hope both in the present and in the future.

It is essentially a truism that while one in a time of bravado and health often ignores the other world, the specter of death is always present, and will be flashed on the screen of reality should life become fragile. In the inner being of all individuals, the question will rise, "What then?" and then again, "Is there any hope for me?" The "me" of the self, the "me" who faces what is really "real," will project the ultimate question.

As Anthony Reading has reaffirmed, "We are the only ones who anticipate life and the future, and death as the ultimate fate."[5] Our challenge is to steer a course whereby we can generate hope in place of despair.

This hope is based on the one who is not only our ultimate cause, but in his infinite power gives us a word from beyond to the now of our lives. A narrow-minded, "Christian only" approach? A prejudiced answer? No, for despite one's specific religious belief, there is that hope for purpose and meaning that logically must come from beyond human comprehension.

In this work, *Sounds of Hope*, we have used the concept of music as the vehicle with which to illustrate the sounds of hope and the need for harmony. Anthony Reading has lent support to our usage of this theme when he noted that, "Music has a unique ability to evoke emotion and humor . . . with certain conditions making us feel joyful and at other times sad."[6]

In a world so filled with emptiness and devoid of the power of hope, very often we need a new sound, a symphonic sound of hope. The rich resources that reach beyond the greatest technological advances are available in something so well-known as music. How often have we, in whatever circumstances we find ourselves, heard a note, a sequence of sounds, yes, literal sounds, that change one's whole feelings toward life and its many distortions? This sound can often be that which initiates new hope, a new way out of the old, the all too popular sounds of despair.

We live in a very concrete, materialistic world. But recently there has been a return to the necessity of the spirit. Life is more than a collocation of atoms. As even the most technological theorist is becoming ever more

5. Reading, *Hope and Despair*, 138.
6. Ibid., 85.

aware that the dynamics of the spirit are not a sojourn into the surreal or an icon of the past, but a core of reality. Thus music, while being so very materialistic in its sounds, has at its real core something more. Certainly this "sound of music" (not the movie) is heard in many ways and has given hope to untold numbers of those who tune in to this sound.

How often has one's inner spirit been lifted because of a certain sound? Whether that sound comes from a famous symphony or possibly an earnest but untrained performer, "something happens," and we are never the same. This sound, whatever and wherever its origin, can make us sad or joyful.[7]

While this may be sound that initiates sadness, this very sound may at the same time reach our inner being and elicit a joy once submerged, waiting to be heard. How vividly I remember in CPE (Clinical Pastoral Education), when trying to avoid sadness, my very avoidance had stifled notes of joy that I would have heard had I "tuned in." It is said, as the late Henri Nouwen often noted, we often suffer to bring hope to bear in life's dark places. But out of these dark places, hope can arise, and, by its sound, it can shed light on a once dark situation.

In any musical score, there can be notes of a minor or major key, and it is this very combination that can give harmony in what would appear to be discord. Because of this new sound, a sound of hope, arising out of the depths, a joyous note can and will be heard. All too often our inner sense hears only the fearful sounds of despair which drown out the sound of a new future proclaimed and enacted by our risen Lord as he spoke those poignant words, "Do not be afraid."

While this affirmation is the promise of our risen Lord, there is still the haunting fear permeating both our society and the individuals who are in that society. This fact and its outcome were brilliantly illustrated in a recent article by a Princeton graduate student. In telling of the recent death of a fellow student during heart surgery, and the pain and the loss, he relates how this friend did not fear the operation. As many young theologians trained in CPE have similarly concluded, he concluded that his friend was in denial.

The truth was that his friend did not deny the possibility of death but only its finality. His faith was in the resurrection.[8] Certainly this was

---

7. Ibid., 138.

8. Jones, "In Memory of H. Shulte," 32–34.

the true sound of hope in action. Yes, there is and continues to be pain and pathos in all of life, and this is also, as Moltmann affirms, an end and a new beginning. If one listens to the sound from the one described, the fact becomes very clear that he was aware of the final symphonic product and its beauty despite the raucous sounds of his disease and the surgery that attempted to fix the problem.

We live in a world of sound, both overt and implicit, from many sources, each calling to be heard. Because of so many sounds from multiple directions, it becomes very difficult to ascertain a clear sound of hope. For a society that seems to tune in so frequently to stations of violence and despair, a culture of death has been created. In fact much of what passes for entertainment is a combination of varied portrayals of violence, despair, and death.

To the embarrassment of what passes for the Christian faith, this violence is also deeply engrained in the fiber of its very substance. It would seem then that the one who proclaimed peace and was its very incarnation must have his words tuned out by its professed adherents. His words of hope, again, "Do not be afraid," have, in reality, been relegated to a dusty shelf of musical scores that do not come to life written by pseudo-Christians. Or could this have occurred because some computer programmer merely substituted a "different program?"

If we are to compose a true symphony of hope, this hope must be based on vitalities of faith that exude from its very structure and based on the triple reality of body, mind, and spirit. In Jim Loder's work, *The Transforming Moment*, he has given this writer an exciting truth as illustrated by this need. Life as a whole is not limited in times of extremities. Our lives are not a perpetual series of crisis experiences. In other words, we have daily tasks that, while not dramatic, are necessary for our lives.

But there can be those special moments, as Loder noted, both by his own personal experiences and by the experiences of others, that he called "convictional experiences," and these are events that are transforming moments, moments that change one's life not for the moment, but forever.[9]

Dr. Loder's life was changed by his remarkable recovery after a serious auto accident. He had stopped to aid a motorist and was struck by an oncoming car. As described by Loder, he became aware of the sense of a

9. Loder, *The Transforming Moment*, 4–11.

presence, an assurance that he would be physically healed by a combination of dedicated "pray-ers" and the prayers from churches near and far. This was a convictional experience!

Hope was now a living reality. While skeptics may attempt to mediate such events as coincidental or just being an anecdote, such was not the case. Loder was a well-known scholar who would never look at things on the surface only.

While this was deeply embedded into the soul and psyche of Dr. Loder, he was cognizant that too often the established church, of which he was a member and a theologian and faculty member, would be likely to deny his reality. They would acknowledge the physical help he received, but any help beyond this would be suspect to say the least. Yet as Loder further notes, 80 percent of clergy and 50 percent of laity have claimed to have such experiences as he had.

It is experiential events such as these transforming moments or convictional experiences that give us impetus in building a symphony of hope. In a world that is seeking something more than the present, more than the visible, there is still the tendency to lean excessively on the concrete—a strange paradox. But deep within even the most objective-minded person is the desire to go beyond, to be aware of a power and purpose, a hope beyond the now and the finite.

To build a symphony of hope whereby the participants will be in perfect harmony to begin with, each participant will be able to see and use his or her particular ability to affect the desired sound. Our world does need those with a critical, objective mode of thought, and the more mystical, the visionaries, must recognize this. But as in a literal symphony, each must play its part to effectively give a sound of unity, serenity, and symmetry that will project joy and excitement to its listeners.

A world is waiting to hear the true sounds of hope—a hope generated by participants of various sounds that can and will answer the deep questions of life, purpose, and ultimate destiny. This real hope, for which the world awaits, is not an escape from reality or a fictional optimism. Yes, discords will occur. There are sounds of despair which are not comprehensible by our finite minds. Nevertheless, even as we begin to tune the various instruments by participants and the instruments are heard, the pattern will be heard as a master conductor is allowed to lead, to give his direction, and the transformation will begin.

Our world does project many sounds of discord, sounds from that which we often label as both secular and sacred. This separation is, in reality, not a valid concept. All of life is of sacred value, and the world in which we live must come to see the inherent value in all of creation, a creation waiting to be reborn, as noted in the New Testament, e.g., the writings of St. Paul.

Nevertheless, while in reality all true scholarship should be seen only as various avenues to truth and to the transformation of our world, there are sounds coming from diverse fields of study. From the areas of theology we have sounds of hope clearly coming from the minds of Jürgen Moltmann and Wolfhart Pannenberg and their American counterparts, Carl Braaten and Robert Jensen, to name a few. From the halls of learning from the scientific fields come writers such as Polkinghorne and company, and a work by the George Washington University scholar Patrick Glynn entitled *God: The Evidence*. Above and beyond scholarship in these areas, even the hope of heaven, once relegated to being a mythical concept of the past, is now gaining a new sound.

A world apprehensive of the future and its ever intimidating sounds is hoping and listening for such a sound. To the prolific writings of Alistair McGrath, *A Brief History of Heaven* has recently been added. After recently publishing works whereby he plumbs the secrets of God, the universe, and the logic of faith under the titles *The Unknown God* and *Glimpsing the Face of God*, he unapologetically dares to speak of a beyond. As McGrath sets forth his thesis, the human desire for something more than the visible is clearly engraved in the human personality. For McGrath, there is definitely more to life than the present, and there is the hope beyond the closed world of our finite minds. An individual so filled with the tensions both outward and inward is reaching for that "more," but all too often, the answers readily available are only predictions by pseudo-prophets under the guise of Christian fundamentalism.

Meanwhile, earnest individuals who do not concern themselves with perpetual contention between the closed minds of the fundamentalists, who build a theology of despair, hate, and heaven for only their select few, and the revised "modern" approach of a one-world reality are waiting for hope and, yes, quite possibly, the reality of heaven. Once more the question must be asked of those from both areas of thought, "Why are your worlds so closed?"

While this world, so bereft of hope, waits and hopes for something more, the *kerygma,* the good news of purpose here and beyond offered by the risen Christ, is locked away in a closed system, inhabited by both those called fundamentalist and liberal, but real good news can never be totally contained. As previously noted, there are solid sounds of hope and life being played by some of the most solid scientists in the realm of the physical, complementing not only the exciting sounds of theologians, but also psychologists who have dared to become participants in the symphony of hope.

And the symphony, while still in its elementary stages, is being heard in ever increasing intensity.

Change in itself is a given, for to live is to change, and life itself is dependent upon change. However, the pattern of change, a pattern that cannot decrease, is building a world that is not able to envision what kind of structure is being built. The very selfhood of this world is asking in its deeper moments of thought, "What is really 'real'?" In a world that seems to stifle any call for wholeness and stability, the real sounds of hope, of joy, must be heard. Can there be a sound in our present that will not be merely a hollow sound in our halls of loneliness? Yes, if and when the real basis for hope is found.

Decades ago, the brilliant theologian Paul Tillich shook the theological world with his book entitled *The Shaking of the Foundations* when he proclaimed the shocking fact that human beings can shake the foundations either positively and negatively. It is our choice.[10] This was followed by the companion volume entitled *The New Being,* in which Tillich wrote of the possibility of a new being, a ground that need not be prey to all of the shaking occurring and would be occurring.[11] These works were published more than five decades ago, yet are relevant when we are exploring the need for a new sound, the sound of hope, hope amidst a world of shaky foundations.

The reader will recall that the vital question asked by individuals entering the office of a professional psychologist was, "Do you have any hope?" This question is sounded again and again by my students of today, both old and young, for while the call for hope and purpose may be only implicitly uttered, the overt lives portray the tension, the very visible quest

10. Tillich, *The Shaking of the Foundations,* 8.

11. Tillich, *The New Being,* 138.

for a new sound, the sound of hope. At the community college where I am an adjunct professor of psychology, the picture of this need is evident. My students range from advanced high school students taking early college courses to grandparents trying to keep up in a fast-changing world, but all have a universal call and question, "Give us hope!" and "Is there any hope in a world that cannot understand?"

The question of "What is Life?" and the "why" of its existence may be easily labeled as existential questions. Yet while the term "existential" may be meaningless to the average person, the fact remains that everyone is asking the question of the "why" of existence. Hope becomes the only real and valid answer if we look at its dynamic and impact on persons in their world, a world ever listening for a sound of hope.

In a world filled with skepticism, it is very easy to negate the concept of hope. If life is in process with few or no major problems, even death is often seen as just a normal sequence of life . . . until a close loved one or one's self faces death's terminating power. As Dr. Loder has noted in his convictional encounter, there are events beyond the norm, the concrete. Facing death, he realized anew that reality is more than what is seen with finite vision. Despite his Harvard doctorate, this individual recognized that there is something not explained by human terms. There is another dimension, which he encountered as he faced death. He was never the same after this convictional event.

The discussion in an academic seminar or in a group of sophisticated young scientists is far different from the apprehension of death in real life. This writer witnessed the radical change that occurred when a young colleague experienced the sudden death of a parent. The whole concept of life and the future was dramatically changed and made more real. This situation was clearly experienced by the writer who had led a discussion with this highly trained scientist-to-be. A future atomic scientist learned of his father's sudden demise at the dinner table. A call was made not to his graduate advisor but to me, his former pastor, just out of Princeton graduate school. The tone of this very brilliant young scientist was one of fear and anger at life, and he was filled with apprehension of the question, "What now?" Now the once ignored occurrence of death became a real element with which to deal. This event, which could be noted as only one anecdote, was more than that. It was illustrative of the perpetual need for hope. The young man would seek at least a partial answer, yet one that alone would not suffice.

It is to such situations that Moltmann's work *In the End—the Beginning* becomes relevant. In stark contrast to too many popular theologians and frothy books of devotion written by those who live on the surface, Moltmann's work speaks a word that writes a new picture of life and death in his concept of the reality of hope eternal. Moltmann, who found reality in life after the horrendous events of World War II while serving as a teenage soldier, wrote from real experience. Life is more than a temporary respite from death. In the end is a new beginning, not for a chosen few, but for all of creation, of which we are a part.

A world that so quickly turns to the extreme of a narrow fundamentalism or a "new old" mode of modernism must encounter a true eschatology, or doctrine of the future. In essence, our society has allowed the concept of eschatology to be relegated to the realm of sensationalism. Our world now, as always, awaits a new beginning, and only a new beginning can transform a world so out of tune. The players of the symphony, for which this world waits so anxiously to hear, can and will be assembled and play a tune of harmony and purpose. A sound of true spirituality will not be affected until all areas of study can be seen in their intended roles.

From the New Age followers to the radical wing of self-appointed prophets and countless others, the concept of eschatology has become an anathema. Nevertheless, we cannot really envision what life is about unless a valid concept and usage of the term "eschatology" is obtained. The question is ever before us, "What is beyond?" The "now"—the present—is never enough.

Pseudo-answers are easily available by movies, TV, novels, etc., along with the religious radicals from both the right and the left. While these answers are disseminated, even by politicians and leaders of our own "enlightened" nation, the world calls for answers. The answers offered are only answers echoing from the hollow caverns of despair, a despair too frequently designed by those who carry religious labels, Christianity included.

The question that then must be faced regarding politics is, "Is there a need for religion and politics to be in partnership?" Once more the proper adage is, "Don't talk about religion or politics if you want to have a peaceful conversation," yet nothing could be further from the truth. Religion is our ultimate concern, as Tillich said decades ago, and politics are how we live; in other words, our policies occur whether or not we recognize them as guiding our lives. Does this mean that we need a theocracy? Certainly not! While we have endured the presence of the "moral majority" (which was often neither moral nor the majority), and we have seen leaders of both parties claim to be God-anointed. This is not the answer.

Our world, a world of multiple faiths, is seeking to hear and experience sounds of harmony, and this world so permeated with fear waits to hear the words of the risen Lord, "Do not be afraid." Does this mean that only we of the Judeo-Christian faith have an avenue to these words? Again, certainly not! For while we can unapologetically affirm our risen Christ, could it not be that others with different terms and words are still able to hear the word of hope, the word that will write new chapters of hope in all of God's creation?

This new sound of hope, the sound of a symphony of hope, can and will be heard if and when all participants begin to play in the key of hope—hope for all creation. For even the most articulate soloists can never play a whole symphony; only a collective aggregate of individuals following one conductor will be able to project a harmony this discordant creation so deeply needs.

Dante has literarily described hell as the place where there is no escape or hope, but as Moltmann so incisively proclaims, hell is no longer inescapable. How and why? Because the living Christ has the keys of hell and the gates are open. Happily, Christ has not lost the key, as traditional theology seems to assume.

In a devastating assault on the traditional concept of hell which, as Moltmann notes, is like a religious torture chamber, exceeding the worst that mortal tyrants could conceive. This world, which is so terribly broken, hearing so many sounds of despair, does not need to hear a future that only emits sounds of gloom and doom. A hurting society, as only blank pages, awaits the writing of a new score of hope. A theology and psychology of hope will be the medium that writes new notes of hope. The conductor now waits for all participants of life to join the symphony of hope.

Perhaps there are few if any scholars in the contemporary American theological scene more qualified to play in this symphony of hope than Carl Braaten. In his exciting works in the area of a theology of hope, and in his work in dialogue with not only mainstream Protestantism but the Roman Catholic church as well, one sees his qualifications to be a real participant in the symphony of hope.

After years as possibly America's leading theologian from the late 1960s to the present, he is now building bridges between the once almost insurmountable chasm between the Catholic church and Protestantism. In his work entitled *Mother Church: Ecclesiology, and Ecumenism,* Braaten, a solid Lutheran with a firm Christology, makes this ground-breaking statement, "To affirm that God revealed Himself uniquely in Jesus Christ does not deny that God has communicated to all people something of his eternal power and deity in the things that have been made (Romans 12). In a sense that must be carefully defined, there is a universal revelation of God that can be known apart from God's conversation with Israel."[12] A statement such as this would certainly shake the foundations of closed orthodoxy and would initiate a new view of God's transcendence over all creation.

How often have not only theologians and pastors but laity as well wondered if and where those "others" were in God's revelation and proclamation of the kingdom in the risen Christ. Too often earnest Christians are seen to project an elitism or a feeling that all the world's wrong: "except thee and me, and I sometimes wonder about thee!" But if we seek to build a true symphony of hope, there may be instrumentalists who can and will bring a new and melodious sound to a symphony never heard before.

Reading Braaten's affirmation of God's revelation reaching all does not in any way negate a strong emphasis on the living Christ. His tone of universalism does not diminish the power of the Christ, but examined in context, enhances God's revelation in Christ.[13] Thus to this writer, God's power and outreach is envisioned beyond that which to so many is a restricted and limited reach. To read Braaten is to read one who is adding a fresh new sound to a symphony of hope.

In the monumental work *The End of the World and the Ends of God,* new contemporary sounds of hope are set forth in an exciting eschatology. For too long, the reality of eschatology has been ignored by those in the academic realms of theology and psychology and, of course, within the scientific community. Rather, this area has been the province of radicals both right and left.

Sensationalism, complete with all-knowing predictions, has been the main view of eschatology in our world, and partly because of this,

---

12. Braaten, *Mother Church: Ecclesiology and Ecumenism,* 120.

13. Braaten and Jenson, *The Futurist Option,* 89.

mainstream society, both secular and religious, along with the scientific community, has either lost interest or relegated its concept to an archaic past. However, with new studies regarding the cosmos along with exploration into the microcosmic creation, eschatology is now another "in" along with the once dismissed concern with spirituality. In a world so fraught with fear, the search for meaning and a hope beyond the finite and the "now of life" is in process.

Whereas a few short years ago, the mention of a spiritual dynamic would be met with disdain, such is no longer the situation. Not only leading theologians, philosophers, and psychologists, but the scientific community including cosmologists, are taking another look. Perhaps there is more to reality than our myopic vision has given us. A new score of harmony is now in process. As Polkinghorne has stated, "In a dialogue between science and theology, both sides should demonstrate their advocacy of truth, showing that this is not a simple task, but one that must contend with many vague and simplistic answers offered from both sides."[14]

Our concern with and goal of building a new symphony of hope has been to initiate a dialogue whereby each field shares its concept of reality and the truth this engenders. Truth, despite what postmoderns strive to deny, is still a relevant reality. The problem seems to be that truth must be seen from more than one perspective. As put forth throughout this work, a symphony must have multiple instruments to produce the sound conceived by its composer. Hope, then, in its many facets and potential, must be envisioned likewise. The amazing fact is evident that despite the reality of modern physics, whereby for decades matter and energy are known to be interchangeable, both proponents seem to deny the reality of the other. In other words, authoritarianism in both fields of material and spiritual, have a barrier regarding what is "really real."

An ever-expanding quest for understanding the physical essence of reality is certainly a valid endeavor, and the element of the mystical, the spirit, must be incorporated if the wholeness of reality is to be projected. A society that in the not-too-distant past had focused almost entirely on the concrete, which the logical positivists labeled as "real," is now finding a vacuum in life. Fear of the present and future, generated not only by those labeled terrorists but by the very universe in which we live brings

14. Polkinghorne, *The End of the World*, 8.

the question, "Do we live in a friendly universe or are we only an occurrence on a minute planet in one corner of an engulfing universe, a universe which is only one of many?"

It is with such seemingly unanswerable questions that any seeker of truth and reality must wrestle. As emphasized throughout this work, if hope is only a temporary respite in a world, a universe, destined for extinction, then all of our exploration in the humanities and sciences themselves are merely exercises in futility.

How relevant then was a song by Peggy Lee, a singer of the not-too-distant past, who in a haunting melody asked, "Is that all there is?" While the song told of her life of boredom, the question "Is that all there is?" is the question of everyone if this finite life is the sum total of life in reality. This is not all there is if we begin to build a symphony of hope, a hope that can and will make a new melody, a new sound, above the cacophony of our present world.

If we look beyond our finite vision above the discords of life with its tangled webs of despair, we can see and hear a sound from another land, as Ben Campbell Johnson has said so vividly. We do live in a world of sight and sound, and to hear the often quiet sounds of hope is never easy. Yet amidst the sounds of hate, violence, and death, we can and will hear that sound from another land. Why? Because the God of creation and the power of the risen Lord is still speaking and desiring to lead us to a harmony—a new sound of a symphony of hope.

To watch drivers in passing cars, as well as students walking across college campuses, is to see communication in action, for cell phones are almost literally their ears. In the world in which we live, so lonely, so filled with apartness, whether in a fast-moving vehicle or on a campus, that sound must be heard. The question comes to this writer, "Why in a world of such sophisticated communications do we fail to really know each other?" No, it is not wrong, nor should we ignore the latest and relevant means of communication (now we have the iPhone, etc.), but is it not important to explore what and why we are communicating? Do we really seek to send out some sounds of hope? Do we try to tune in on the frequency of caring, love, and the hope that initiates a new reality? Our society, our world, is so lonely and out of tune, and will continue to be, until the new sound of hope can be communicated.

The marvel of our electronic communications is increasingly awesome. Yet could it not be, as Robert Jensen has noted, that our prayer makes a claim that is also tremendous?[15] In fact, prayer lays claim to being a co-determiner of the universe. Certainly this is the epitome of daring to communicate beyond the scope of the electronic world.

In a world so filled with loneliness, where individuals send out silent cries for help, electronic devices are not enough. While individuals check e-mail, voice mail and text messages, deep within they desire to hear the sound of hope. This hope, while an element for persons of every endeavor, from the homemaker to the scientist, initiates the need for achievement, e.g., "I hope this turns out right," etc. Deep within the inner self, there is always a feeling of seeking another way, a way out of our hurts, our tendency to despair, and the need to be filled with that which initiates a new life, a life of purpose, which only hope can fulfill.

This need has been, and is being, fulfilled by the ultimate event in history, the resurrection of our Lord. Because of this risen Christ, we can know there is another way, that hope is not an idle dream, but one based, as Moltmann affirms, on the God who comes. Pannenberg, a contemporary of Moltmann, has noted that we have seen the finger of God pointing to a new world of hope, fulfilled because of the Christ event, his incarnation in real life. For a world seeking revelation of the future, this is hope in progress!

Revelation, the future, the unknown, are certainly popular topics for books, TV, movies, and entertainment as a whole. The mystical, the unknown, and even the occult are very much in vogue. As has been noted throughout this work, the person of today lives in a state of apprehension regarding not only the future but the present as well. The question of almost universal significance is, "What is it all about?" or "Why am I here?" Unless one has a true sense of hope, individuals will continue to exist in a vacuum of fear, loneliness, and lack of direction.

In parishes both large and small, rural and urban, one topic that is almost always chosen for Bible study is Revelation. My question is "Why this book?" The answer was the same. While difficult in its mystical symbols and a popular resource for radicals, people desire to know what the world is coming to. A quest for hope, real hope, is always present, whether overtly or implicitly. As earnest individuals seek to find answers in books such as Revelation, the haunting fear of life ending and being meaningless becomes evident.

15. Braaten and Jenson, *The Futurist Option*, 156.

Once more the concept of real hope becomes paramount in the individuals whose lives are constantly bombarded by news of one disaster and tragedy after another and so does the question of "Where is God in all of this, if there is a God to believe in at all?" Yet deep within each person who dares to go inward, an inner being is hoping for something and someone beyond. Beyond the visual, beyond the almost perpetual news of gloom and projections of despair, there is that spark of hope waiting to be generated into a light in the darkness.

The Book of Revelation all too often has been used by pseudo-prophets who offer solid evidence of "just what will happen," and a fearful society too often accepts their answers as revelation usually given as a gift of x amount of dollars. However, there are exciting scholars as noted such as Moltmann and Pannenberg, etc., who have opened real vistas into the book that for many is one of mystery. Only recently the late New Testament scholar Bruce Metzger left this life and certainly now is experiencing revelation firsthand. In one of his last works entitled *Breaking the Code*, Metzger sets forth the key to Revelation when he states, "The intention is to fix the reader's thought not upon the symbol but upon the idea that the symbolic language is designated to convey."[16] That is essentially that there is hope for the future. Here is what revelation is in practical application.

To see God, to see the future, and to hear sounds that will harmonize all of a discordant creation, is not possible in our limited vision of revelation. Nevertheless, we can, as Alistair McGrath cogently notes in his book *Glimpsing the Face of God*, initiate the search for meaning in the universe. In vivid literary expression, McGrath projects the vision of God as seen not only through the mind and eyes of the theologian but through those of the scientist as well.

As McGrath begins to sum up the logic and the vision of God's revelation, he states the question and answer when he says, "Something lies beyond the horizon of our experience and beckons us onward to discover it, and by doing so we enter into the greatest discovery that life can offer."[17] In closing his work, McGrath says, "We are but wayfarers wandering in the lonely night, who see dimly upon the distant mountain peak a sun that never rises here but which will never set in the new heavens

16. Metzger, *Breaking the Code*, 66.
17. McGrath, *Glimpsing the Face of God*, 123.

thereafter. And this is enough. It comforts and cheers us on our dark and rugged way."[18]

The average person's life, with its pressures of daily survival, is enough to occupy one's time. Then a crisis occurs, either personally or in the life of a loved one. Suddenly, the "now" of life is not enough. The emptiness facing the person, the apprehension of the unknown, becomes very real, and the encounter with the eschatological moment, bringing new unknowns into one's life, occurs. Human beings do think about life, its purpose, and the future.

For those who are old enough to remember the Cold War, the not-forgotten fear of nuclear war hovered over all. Presently this is replaced by the constant threats of terrorism, by a real or a purposeful fear generated by politicians. From whatever or wherever the source lies, the need for a sense of life beyond this life, beyond our finite concept, is present. Until this is met, we are, as Tillich noted decades ago, in a state of existential loneliness. We look at the world and the universe, and we are struck with the fear that perhaps we are all alone in an uncaring, unloving universe. Centuries before Tillich's proclamation, the ancient words of the Hebrew writer in Ecclesiastes 3:11 came to bear upon our situation, "He has put eternity in the hearts of humanity."

Jim Loder, in one of his last treatises before his untimely death, affirmed the fact that within the real human being is a built-in sense of an awareness of the transcendent; in other words, we are constructed for life eternal. In Loder's words, "Death stops the heartbeat, but it does not quench the human spirit. It is inherent logic that tells us that there is a way to transcend and transform death."[19]

Certainly if a true symphony of hope is to be composed, its very essence must be constructed with, and from, eternal notes. A further addition to Loder's concept regarding transcendence is in his statement that affirms, "The universe owes its existence to a personal Author greater than we can conceive."[20] Then by following Loder's train of thought, it is only logical that what we designate as matter, as the concrete, was first formed by spirit. This spirit comes from the author who creates matter out of his word.

18. Ibid.
19. Loder, *The Logic of the Spirit*, 4.
20. Ibid.

Richard Cox, in his groundbreaking work *The Sacrament of Psychology*, has noted that "'hard scientists' who disavowed the existence of any 'supreme being' a few years ago . . . now admit the possibility. Others have completely changed their minds and are now firm believers, even Theists, many Christian Theists at that."[21] Richard Cox is not one who denies any valid sign of the advances, as he is both an MD and a theologically trained psychologist. Essentially what Dr. Cox is saying is that too often modern psychologists and logical positivists have negated the greatest source of help, the living God as seen in his son Jesus Christ.

As this writer is striving to set forth a symphony of hope whereby multiple disciplines can work together, Cox's ideas are very relevant as we can begin to see each "instrument" contributing its specific sound of hope.

One of the most exciting occurrences in the various fields of study is the recognition of the similarities in the goals of each, specifically healing. Whether we turn to the medical fields, social studies, mental health, and/or religion in its many expressions, each desires to affect healing. The healing of a wounded society, and, yes, even the earth on which we live, cannot occur until health is achieved for the totality of life.

For too long we have sought to heal physical bodies via the best scientific methods, and we have worshiped at the shrine of multiple approaches to the human mind. These present and past attempts to heal individuals are an exercise in futility unless we have a cosmological vision and a plan for our planet's very existence. Our very environment is not only threatened by the conflicts of various societies, by our continual rape of the earth and its atmosphere, generated by the loss of true values, values which are not transient, regardless of postmodern views. Change must not be compromised with the possibility of absolute truth.

Cox notes that Ursula Anderson, a leading authority in many of the aforementioned fields, has given much credence to the power of the "biology of the soul" and the reality of the spirit in her most recent research.[22] For Anderson, we need to unashamedly initiate a revision of theology that can and will affect almost unimaginable achievement in the physical and psychological sciences. In essence, what the leaders in these multiple areas of learning are telling us is that we in the area of religion and theology

21. Cox, *The Sacrament of Psychology*, 290.
22. Ibid., 290–91.

must dare to set loose our unused potential. This healing could be, and to a degree has been, used in the cures even of such killer diseases as cancer. As Dr. Cox takes us another step, and as Anderson has intimated, we need invasive theology. Yes! This is quite a blow to the logical positivists who accept only laboratory proofs. Once more we are beginning to see the primacy of the spirit, of the mystical, before the concrete and the visible.

A world that is out of tune and afraid to hope is finally beginning to listen to the timeless sound of hope coming from the creator who has the key to real and total health. As the alchemists centuries ago sought to find the key to rebuild our world back to Eden, perhaps our present society can begin to play in the universal key that can and will bring harmony to a discordant world. We need to once more envision the possibility of a world, a universe, that is expressed in a unity, in a sense of wholeness. Only by building a true symphony of hope can we begin to bring harmony and beauty to a world that too often resigns itself to living not only "quiet lives of desperation," but noisy lives of destruction.

In the life of every thinking human being lies a silent question of what is beyond, beyond our finite vision and our closed worldviews. While this may never be verbalized, the real problem, the real question, is still there.

From the newest work of Brian Greene entitled *The Fabric of the Cosmos*, we see at least a quiet sound of his thoughts regarding the future of science: "It is an entertaining and constructive exercise."[23] He further states that "when such speculation turns to the future of space-time itself, it takes on an almost mystical quality; we're considering the fate of the very things that dominate our sense of reality . . . [R]egardless of future discoveries, space and time will continue to frame our individual experience; space and time, as far as everyday life goes, are here to stay. What will continue to change, and likely change drastically, is our understanding of the framework they provide . . ."[24]

To read Greene is to see one who is open to new concepts of reality— in stark contrast to all too many theologians and/or pseudo-scientists. As Greene noted, "Physicists spend a large part of their lives in a state of

23. Greene, *The Fabric of the Cosmos*, 492.
24. Ibid.

confusion. It's an occupational hazard. To excel in physics is to embrace doubt while walking the winding road to clarity."[25]

In our composing a symphony of hope, it is so very important that, while believing the outcome of faith and hope, we must recognize our human limitations, our inability to know "all" regarding the future. Even physicists, who in spite of their incomparable advances in their under-standing of the exploration of the space-time challenge, still recognize that their knowledge is limited. So, too, can we see new openings of what hope can and does offer.

How refreshing to see one with the mind such as that of Greene be-ing reverent and open to what reality is and how much is yet unknown. If, as has been noted throughout this work, a true symphony of hope can be written, its score must include all valid concepts from each field of study in order to affect a true sound of hope.

Our world, our earth, is not a fluke of nature, as many logical positiv-ists would claim. The late cosmologist Carl Sagan would probably agree with that idea. The earth, the world in which we live, contains multiple layers of reality just below the surface. How can this be verified? Simply by looking at life not only panoramically, but with a microcosmic vision along with an awareness of the vast cosmos and an awareness that at best we see only partially. Music, beauty, love, and purpose are not measur-able in a scientific laboratory, but only by experience—experience that is always more than can be expressed in the concrete. A world with so many unanswered questions is ever a challenge, but the very challenge tells us that there is a goal, a horizon, to be envisioned. The symphony of hope, our goal in life, is not to be limited to the past, the present, or even the future, but would be played in what Tillich designated as the "eternal now." This "now" of our lives is, in essence, the basis of reality, for only in our "now" can we as finite beings project a logical yet mystical concept of hope. Hope as projected in this work is to be an active hope, a hope that moves from merely wishing or fearing extinction, but is ever reaching beyond in confidence. This hope is only guaranteed by the risen Christ who awaits our arrival.

A person is born, lives, and dies, and that is a truism. No philosophy nor the most accurate measurement in science can refute this. Life does have a 100 percent ending, if physical life is all that we are considering.

---

25. Ibid., 470.

But a symphony of hope will go beyond the ending and continue playing beyond the temporary, and the ending will always have a new beginning. In this postmodern world where truth is projected as only relative, the truth of death is not negated. However, if we would be tempted to follow the nihilists, the logical positivists, then "that's all there is."

From the ever creative mind of Carl Braaten, the American hope theologian, comes a solid refutation of those who would dismiss life as only a biological incident. As Braaten points out regarding so-called "modern man," there is little to distinguish him or her from primitive man in the face of death, "I think he's really scared to death of death." While this was written nearly thirty years ago (note the masculine gender), Braaten is still very much a theologian of hope. "Modern man," as Braaten notes, "has nothing to offer to put death to death."[26]

In a recent issue of *The Princeton Seminary Bulletin*, Dr. Powery proclaims the inevitability of death but also its destruction in a poignant sermon entitled "Death Threat." Yes, a threat to death itself! For what we designate and fear as death is itself destined to death.[27]

Why? Powery reminds us that while in this life we negate death and the sorrow it initiates, we know as ever the risen Christ who will come, and life's seeming destruction will give way to power of the resurrection. While we await the final victory when death is destroyed, we must ever focus of all that attacks life.

To return to Powery's powerful message, we hear him proclaim the need for many "deaths!" Yes, death to the division of Republicans and Democrats. Death to the divisions between black, brown and white. Death between rich and poor and those who are different but are God's wholly creation. A creation that calls for life. And this call has been heard by the living Risen Christ.[28]

From the writings of the late Jim Loder, the need for putting death to death parallels the writings of Dr. Powery. In this creative statement, Dr. Loder notes "in Christ death is put to death and the transformation inherent in the human spirit is in itself transformed by the Creative Spirit. This does not mean that the faithful do not die, it means death cannot hold them, so they will live again . . . death does not have the final word."

26. Braaten, *Eschatology and Ethics*, 65.

27. Powery, "Death Threat," 249.

28. Loder, *The Logic of the Spirit*, 140.

In a world so full of words yet so empty of answers, a new word is the only sound that gives hope, a hope that there is another way . . . the way of resurrection! While the world appears to be dying, the fact of the risen Christ's presence writes a new story of life in place of death.

Our world—that shining jewel in a vast universe—is not destined for non-being, because of this one who has written a new story of life with the destiny of hope. The fact that we exist in a culture of death does negate the fact that there is more than existence to our destiny. There is life—life because of the living, risen Christ!

It is this perpetual problem of life and death, with all of its dynamics, that only a true symphony of hope can answer. These sounds are being heard and becoming part of the composition, but certainly not as quickly as desired. Yet as Robert Emmons notes, "We are embarking on a significant period in the scientific study of spirituality. For personality and goal researchers, this means that we will be able to continue to move toward an understanding of the ultimate goals of human existence . . . The goal approach to spirituality shows that we need not compromise scientific rigor and precision in order to make progress in understanding what people find valuable, purposeful, and meaningful."[29]

Certainly, then, whatever our orientation to life and death, the fact remains that both the areas of science and the humanities are vital to answer the hope of all human beings. Perhaps once more theology may be able to lay claim to the once archaic title of "queen of the sciences." Now I am deeply aware that to the modern world, and especially to that labeled postmodern, to put theology above all areas of study would appear to border on the ludicrous. However, if we look at theology as the study of reality, the reality of a creator God and the risen Lord, then this view would seem to have credence.

The areas of theology, cosmology, psychology, are in one sense all based on the spiritual. If we affirm that spirit comes before the material, then logic would lead us to accept the concept of spirit as primary. Then theology would, in a sense, be the primordial source of understanding reality.

A true symphony of hope can only be written and played when each instrument is heard. Tragically enough, a world so out of tune fails to listen to the tones of truth, such as love, compassion, and faith. As Robert

29. Emmons, *A Psychology of Ultimate Concerns*, 178–79.

Emmons has noted, "The biggest threat to understanding is a failure to take seriously those phenomena which make us most human."[30]

Thus we return to the analogy of spirit vs. matter or the physical. It is only when ideas are formed that a harmony of life is created. To build a symphony of hope is to set loose the notes heard from all areas of study. Then and only then will we be able to see and hear for the first time that symphony that since creation has been the music of the stars.

30. Ibid., 179.

Chapter 7

Sounds of Eschatological Hope
in a World of Discord

"IT'S JUST OUT OF tune," says the pianist upon hearing the sound of his or her supposedly excellent piano. Despite the beautiful wood and the keys of fine materials, the proper sound was not to be heard, and despite the marvelous skill of the pianist, there would be only sounds of discord.

Today we live in a world of incomparable beauty. Lush forests, beautiful streams, and lakes abound. While an increasing population is in evidence, there could be enough for all to live in an idyllic situation. Modern technology has initiated achievements once thought impossible, and along with seemingly unlimited resources, there is plenty for all.

But in the midst of this idyllic world, the raucous sounds of discord are heard. From almost all areas, the cry of the hungry echoes over this world of abundance. Above the cries of the hungry, the many "sounds of silence" are muffled by sounds of war. While individuals of all strata of society hurt from within, a gnawing fear of loneliness, fear of the future and present, the literal pain of the wounded and dying, are very evident. A world of beauty and so much potential waits to hear sounds of hope above the discord, the sense of all the wrong keys being struck. Nevertheless, there awaits the possibility of playing a major key of joy in place of the minor key of despair and death. Are there participants who will begin to make new sounds? Can there really be new sounds of hope and joy in this world so out of tune?

Yes, for over two thousand years ago, one came from beyond into the now of a discordant world, and it could never be the same. Because this one from beyond entered this world, a new melody was heard, and that melody has been heard not only by persons in the prime of life and those who seem to be living a life of harmony, but by hurting and dying persons, for whom hope seems to be lost. Why? Because these individuals have accepted a theology of hope based not on the "now" of our lives, but on a new future, a future projected by Moltmann, who proclaims that "in the end, the new beginning." This life of hope is not based on simply a memory, a review of past achievements, but on a freshness of life and a vision of the ever new.

What is really new? Is it the new discoveries of science, biology, and psychology? Or is it one minute exploration and calculations regarding the cosmos, or at least our own universe? In essence, nothing is really new. For we are only beginning to discover what has "always been." A simple analogy was put forth by a Native American, who was quite indignant when told that Columbus discovered America! How can one discover that which was already here?

A world so out of tune is waiting to hear a true sound of hope, a sound of a symphony of hope, where all instruments contribute to make a new sound. The world of academics has attempted to teach another way, while the so-called "real world" moves increasingly into total discord. Discord, even in what was thought to be found in religion, whatever its expression, has often resulted in different sounds of hate and violence by the very proponents of religion. The fear generated by this hate and violence does not only come from that which we term the secular, but from that often misunderstood term "religion."

While a world, a society, tries to call for a return to "old time religion," and prayer breakfasts are held in places of government, old methods of vengeance are still more in vogue. While war and violence, both local and worldwide, have never solved problems, leaders of a so-called Christian nation have rediscovered the same archaic answer. Meanwhile, a world of pain, poverty, and destruction waits and waits to hear a sound of hope above the sounds of death and despair. Only real hope can be that which will heal.

As individuals and as a collective society, we come to many places and things; in fact, we are seemingly always "coming," but to where? The often heard question, so filled with fear, is "What is the world coming to?" Constant news of pathos, of incomparable tragedy, both natural and human-created, are reported over our sophisticated systems of communication. The only answer regarding this question of "What is the world coming to?" must be reversed. The decision that must be made is not

"What is the world coming to?" but who and what are coming to the world. A sound from beyond must be heard.

Our world is, as one astronaut said as he gazed from space, a jewel glowing in a darkened universe. Despite its regnant beauty, one knows that this world is not only polluted by its inhabitants physically but spiritually as well. Love, compassion, and joy are under constant attack. Violence of all kinds seems to reign. Nevertheless, the harmony that came by the arrival of the risen Lord is being heard. Softly, yes, but little by little, growing in vibrant intensity.

From the casual conversation in various neighborhoods to sophisticated graduate seminars and lecture halls, the need for a new sound is evident. As we listen beneath the surface and yet beyond, there will come a sense of a new sound. In the inner self of human beings, there is a built in "antenna" tuned to hearing sounds of harmony. Idyllic speculation? A sojourn into fantasy? An escape from real life? Such antithesis would seem logical in a society of rationalists, but such is not the true wavelength. New discoveries not only in the fields of psychology but in biology and physics are opening new vistas of communication.

The concept that human beings are actually "wired for God" is one of this era's most exciting theories. The anthropomorphic principle once thought to be a return to a pre-scientific world is now being re-examined, and the closed world of the logical positivist is becoming anti-scientific. There are other dimensions to life and to reality. The transcendent is not a figment of primitive imagination. Conferences on spirituality, as noted, are becoming popular in some of our most sophisticated universities, and are not limited to departments of religious studies.

As Moltmann has so clearly affirmed, "It is encouraging not to have to capitulate before the unalterability of conditions and not to give way to sadness, but to remain upright in protest. People who accept the darkness of their lives resist the light of God which drives out the night. Through the powerful, we don't give up and don't give ourselves up. We remain unreconciled and unaccepting in an urgent and deadly world."[1]

Thus, as human beings we are not just machines nor an accidental convocation of atoms, but there is something within us and beyond that initiates a valid and powerful hope. We are not merely wired to exist for

1. Moltmann, *In the End*, 90.

a few short years, but designed for eternity—but eternal life in all of its fullness.

When we ask ourselves or question society as a whole as to the "why" of discord, of the raucous sounds of hate and death, only one encompassing answer can be given: the world of pain and suffering has negated its true core of spirit and bowed to the god of the visible.

In the turbulent era of the 1960s, perhaps culminated in the year 1968, a year designated by the news media as "a crack in time," a call for help was never really heard. Despite the mass media coverage and cries from both the right and left, this call, even now, has not been heard, and professing Christians remain unmoved.

Our nation moved through the 70s and, despite the Kent State tragedy, seemed to forget or submerge the real need, a call for hope. A call for the transcendent was answered erroneously but honestly by an escape via the drug culture. While the establishment worried about possible anarchy occurring, few individuals sought to hear the unheard cries for meaning of which Viktor Frankl spoke.

Once again, Moltmann gives us a valid and hopeful answer to our dilemma when he says, "before we can change and improve our evil world, we must change and improve ourselves."[2] Yes! We must look within ourselves and then to that which is beyond and hear what the spirit has been saying all along. Our visible world cannot be healed by violence, however efficient violence appears to be.

The war in Iraq is only symbolic of the real problem. We do not see answers in the spirit and seek to have peace by destroying those who are not "us." Now I am deeply aware that the Iraq War and other conflicts are real and not merely symbolic, but they are symbolic by their very nature. So-called Christian nations, including our own, have negated the spirit, the sense of love and hope proclaimed by the risen Christ, and have returned to the god of power.

In such an era, in such a world, the eschatological notes must be heard. The future which always seems so far away has become our "now" and now, as always, is in the process of becoming the past. As the Reformed scholar Hendrikus Berkhof has incisively noted, "The opposition between the old and the new man is a question not of chronology but a

2. Moltmann, *In the End*, 91.

way of existence, not a horizontal but a vertical event."[3] Could it be that the horizontal has trumped the vertical, and this is the reason for our world being so out of tune?

A true harmony in music must be the result of either a plan or a specific ability to play and make harmony by "ear" and not by organized notes. In a very discordant world, we need to review our perception and direction and connection. Our connections have been all too strongly based on what we designate as real, that which is visible and tangible. Now with the so-called real creation beginning to crumble by global warming, ethnic cleansing, and yes, wars of liberation, human beings are beginning to look above. Yes, above the mundane, the closed world of their own making, a world waiting, waiting for something or someone.

Whether the waiting one is a casual thinking religious person, a vibrant believer, or a total skeptic, there is that cry, either overtly or implicitly, for a sound of hope. Hope cannot be created out of mere matter, but must be generated by that primary element of creation, the spirit within. For Berkhof, everything points to the future, but also everything urges us to expect a real future that will mean worldwide resurrection.[4]

Now as always, this world is in need of resurrection. In reality, we live, as Dr. Schuller recently said, in a dying world: "For we normally speak of this world as the land of the living, but in reality it's the land of the dying. But as we look to both a present and future resurrection, it is that other world that is a living world."[5] As any physician knows, ultimately there is no cure for death or illness. At best we can only hold off death longer, and we can help the ill to feel and live better, but in the end, death scores 100 percent. A dire statement? Not really, if we look to the true eschatological aspect of life. It will be as Moltmann so vividly proclaims, "In the end, the beginning."

How often as a child I heard my grandparents speak or sing, "You will understand it better 'by and by.'" Even new Southern gospel tunes are gaining in popularity (and price!). Were the songs of my grandparents' era an escape from a hard life? Possibly, but there was a deep sense that this life was not all. Now perhaps the popularity of contemporary Southern gospel is also an escape.

3. Berkhof, *Well-Founded Hope*, 82.

4. Ibid., 35.

5. Schuller, *Don't Throw Away Tomorrow*, 166.

Nevertheless, whatever the underlying reason for songs that tell of another world, where there is a note of escape being sounded, something must initiate the need to escape. In reality, our sophisticated society, as that of past eras, is trying to escape from pain, despair, and death. Too often, despite the need to escape, to find a light in the darkness, many remain in the "cave" of which Plato speaks. In other words, humans often stay in the dark, because they fear going into the new, the light that awaits them, a new world of light and beauty. Too many become accustomed to the dark!

From contemporary books to movies, the themes are too often ones of violence, pathos, and death. As noted earlier, so-called Christian books often tell of doom, destruction, etc., for all of those "left behind." A sense of fear, of hopelessness, is so very real despite the calling of Christians to be bearers of hope, which Donald Capps has written about in his book *Agents of Hope*. Perhaps the agency has limited its hours or is on the verge of closing! And outside, customers are waiting!

To become a true agent of hope, whether clergy, professional, or laity, one cannot live in a one-dimensional world, for to hope is to dream, to plan, to initiate activities beyond the visible. Whether one is a religious person or not is not the challenge. Once more drawing on Tillich's concept of religion as being one of "ultimate concern," we must go beyond the present, the visible, if the ultimate in any area of concern is to be dealt with.

This is the "why" of our inserting eschatology as the doctrine of the future as a necessity. For now as always, every person, in his or her deeper moments of thought, thinks beyond the visible, the mundane. The "one world at a time" or "pie in the sky" are narrow or satirical expressions of a past era. But as a psychology professor and former therapist for thirty-two years, I have encountered as many or more persons who are not church members as those who are who ask the "whys" of life. The quest for meaning has always been a factor in the lives of individuals in every area of life.

As Robert Emmons has noted, there is empirical evidence of need for meaning in life: "While some philosophers have cooled to the topic of meaning in life, social scientists have been warming to it . . ."[6] Society as a whole seems to have lost meaning, but its constituents are now reengaged in the quest for meaning, and we must remember that all of society is

6. Emmons, *The Psychology of Ultimate Concerns*, 144–45.

made up of individuals. While society and its philosophers may negate the value of meaning, it is the individual who looks and waits for the coming of hope, a hope that must reach ever beyond the "now," the visible, the finite, in order to succeed.

In a world that is increasingly becoming a throw-away society, the need for something to hold onto and that speaks of a kind of permanence is called for. No, the term permanence is hardly accepted, especially in a postmodern world, but there remains an element within the human being that does reach for a permanent love, a permanent hope that gives one another way. To see and initiate another way out of the laboratory of confusion and hopelessness, the other world, the new dimension of life, must be dealt with and reached for, but our reach would be limited to our finite reach unless the risen Christ reaches down to us. Then we know that there is hope, hope incarnate in the living Christ who was and is the true dynamic of hope.

Across time, human beings of all eras and cultures have continued the quest for a hereafter. From the most ancient cultures, the search for life and its non-ending have been both a barrier and a benefit of incalculable proportions. Too often individuals see barriers as a necessary inconvenience, but in reality, they can be a stimulant to achievement in almost all areas of life. This stimulant has resulted in extraordinary achievements in science, literature, travel, and certainly medicine. As noted earlier, however, medicine and all achievements in this area are still temporary, as death still wins.

Nevertheless, it is a seemingly insurmountable barrier to the continuation of life that draws us to the infinite, the future, the sense of desiring harmony despite the discords of life, the loudest of which is death. It is here that the dynamics of an eschatology become relevant, and this relevance is not a form of escapism or sublimation, nor a return to a fantasy of childhood or a pre-scientific world.

In the works of the Helmut Thielicke, a working theologian who tested his theology in both World Wars I and II and later conflicts, we hear a solid note of harmony in looking at, and listening to, a discordant world. Seeing death in its most hideous forms and magnitude drove Thielicke to a conclusion far beyond a graduate seminar or lectures about death.

Being aware of the death of his loved ones and also the masses around him carved an indelible mark on Thielicke's person and psyche. As he poignantly notes, "Every death was and is personal. It is always an

'I' who dies and not a group, a collection of 'I's."[7] Death is terrible when seen as being impersonal and looked upon as a collective event. To see a collection of individuals is to see a unit and not persons. To list casualties as groups too often and easily causes us to forget the "I" of each death.

How easily our society, our world, makes its shelter and security in not knowing the individual, but that unknown individual was once a person designed by his or her creator to play his or her role in the symphony of hope. However, as Moltmann would say, there will be ultimate healing because "in the end is the beginning," and God will restore all of creation. Meanwhile, the destruction goes on.

A life is always in process, and that process is composed of the past and the present, and lurking toward the future. However, the future is a "not yet," and because of this, all we have is the present. Nevertheless, now as always, human beings look ahead, and the future is that which is either positive or negative. As we listen to the sounds around us, harmony and a joyous melody seem almost nonexistent. Each day seems to be only a mark on the calendar of a life in process, but how and what is its purpose?

In the insightful words of Viktor Frankl, there can be, and is, a purpose wherever we find ourselves. Having survived the horror of the Nazi death camps, Frankl found meaning among the confines of unspeakable horror. Yes, meaning where there seemed to be none! Experiences that Dr. Frankl faced culminated in a new approach to psychology that he labeled logotherapy. Speaking about death, Frankl has said, "What is left and what remains is the self, the spiritual self."[8]

Now I am deeply cognizant that with Dr. Frankl being of the Jewish faith, his concept of eternal life and/or resurrection may differ widely from my own beliefs as a Judeo-Christian. However, despite the reality of theological differences, Frankl's acceptance and recognition of the self and the spiritual are very closely related to the Christian concept of the self. As has been known for decades, his theory of logotherapy (or existential analysis) has been, and continues to be, widely used by not only Christian-orientated psychologists, but those in the secular field as well.

Perhaps as we study Moltmann's answers to the question of eternity, one can see both similarities and divergences between his and Frankl's views. As Moltmann notes, "It is *this* transitory life which will

7. Thielicke, *Living with Death*, 143.
8. Frankl, *The Unheard Cry*, 112.

be transformed into eternal life, it is *this* earthly life which will be raised to eternal life . . . God the Creator remains faithful to his creation and its redemption . . . [h]e doesn't give anything up for lost and destroys nothing he has made."[9] In Viktor Frankl's concept of eternity we see a statement that "everything is eternal. More than that, it becomes eternal of itself. We don't have to do anything about it."[10]

The contrast seems to be that for Moltmann, God will take care of all of God's creation, while for Frankl, the creation itself is eternal. Yet in spite of whatever differences remain between Moltmann and Frankl, there is one common thread: they both have a deep awareness of a creator and of themselves being designed by that creator for a purpose. Until individuals, and a society composed of individuals, find purpose and meaning, life is only a state of existence, not living!

We live in a world composed of two dimensions and/or content: matter and energy. Although history records human beings specifically in one or the other, modern physics since Einstein has recognized their unity. Nevertheless, despite modern knowledge, the recognition of each as being interchangeable is all too infrequent. The logical positivists, following on the heels of rationalism, have all but negated any element that is not laboratory-proven. The reality of the spirit is relegated to be an icon of the past, while those who honor the spiritual often ignore the physical.

To look at creation and the incomparable magnitude of space is to see both in harmonious function. Yes, the universe is still in process. So are its individuals! Our challenge is to envision both panoramically and analytically the possibility of harmony between spirit and matter.

Until we as individuals and as society find purpose and meaning in life, we will remain in an existential vacuum. That vacuum can be alleviated only when an eschatological vision is accepted. Human beings are spiritual beings, living in physical structures, in a world composed of both. The importance of this may be seen in this quote of Albert Einstein, "The man who regards his life as meaningless is not merely unhappy, but hardly fit for life."[11] While this sounds overly severe, nevertheless it emphasizes the fact that we need meaning in all of life. Our challenge is to

---

9. Moltmann, *In the End*, 160–61.

10. Frankl, *The Unheard Cry*, 111.

11. Quoted in Schuller, *Don't Throw Away Tomorrow*, 166.

recognize, as Frankl points out, "Unless life points to something beyond itself, survival is pointless and meaningless. It is not even possible."[12]

Eschatology is not an escape, but deals with what Frankl and Elie Wiesel dealt with. As Frankl noted regarding the overall importance of a future orientation, "Only those who were orientated toward the future, toward a goal in the future, toward a meaning to fulfill in the future, were likely to survive."[13] To each of us, fearing as always physical death, the specter of terrorism is paramount. Perhaps the terrorism that we fear, and justifiably so, is that created by our fear of others who are different, and who look upon us as the promoters of terrorism in their lives and their homes. The discord increases whenever and wherever we fail to look beyond our finite power to the power of peace and the hope that is around us.

The late Mother Theresa had, throughout her life, encouraged those in tension and trouble to look above for the answer. Too often, however, the majority of even Christians look to humans, to the horizontal, not the vertical and the eternal.

Meanwhile, with frequent terror alerts, we in our western "Christianized" world, continue to see problems through the myopic eyes of fear instead of seeing the promise of hope. Discord? Yes, but there can and will be harmony when all begin to play sounds of hope, when each instrumentalist plays in the key of love. It is then that the true symphony of hope will be heard. The audience of a discordant, hurting world awaits to hear this new sound. The refreshing news of new sounds of hope is often not coming from those who profess to be followers of the Prince of Peace. Instead, sounds of love and hope are echoing both symbolically and literally from rock stars, the entertainment world, sports celebrities, and yes, even billionaires. Reaching out to the millions around the world with hands of caring, giving bed nets to mosquito-infested areas: these are extensions of the hands of the risen Lord. While these real sounds of hope are being heard, conservative Christians are campaigning against gay marriages, gay rights, and miniscule theological differences. Could it be that the real reason for so many discordant sounds being heard in a world calling for hope is our misplaced values? Perhaps instead of striving to play the melody written by the composer of hope, too many would-be

12. Frankl, *The Unconscious God*, 139.
13. Ibid.

instrumentalists are merely polishing their instruments or deciding who is the most talented or gifted participant.

While there are so many pseudo-Christians, pseudo-intellectuals, and almost everything in between, the good news of hope is being heard and is in process. As noted earlier, the sounds are often quiet and difficult to hear amidst the raucous sounds of hate and despair, but new and true sounds are being heard. From the continuing work for peace being affected by former president Carter and his institute for peace, and other similar groups such as the Mennonite Christian Peacemaker Teams, there are sounds of hope.

The late Donald Juel of Princeton Theological Seminary noted that a word from beyond was the only answer to life and death. "Such hope springs not from interpretative schemes but from a word that must be spoken to us from outside—finally, from God. That such words are spoken and do give life is reason for confidence that death and futility are not the end. That such words can be spoken in ordinary human systems of signs is an indication that the world subject to futility is still vulnerable to the intrusion of a God who raises the dead."[14]

Yes, a power, a presence from outside ourselves, is our ultimate basis for hope. We are not limited to the power within the finite world, for the presence and the power from beyond is available. Yet it is easy to ignore, forget, or even deny this presence. This power is still waiting to be unleashed in a world in need of another presence, another power. To quote again a former professor of mine, from a seminary lecture, "The greatest embarrassment in heaven will be to find out how much power was available and how little we availed ourselves of it."[15]

As I write this, TV and newspapers tell almost casually of many deaths in Iraq, along with new murders locally and nationally. Unless it is a death of local or well-known person, life moves on with hardly a break in its rapidity. Discords in life, those from death, destruction, and numerous other events are hardly noticed. Without realizing it, discord becomes the normal sound instead of the harmony for which our world was designed.

But hope is still the answer. For only when hope is unleashed can any real change, let alone, transformation, occur. Hope, even in a discordant

14. Juel, "Christian Hope," 182.

15. Mendel Taylor, Lecture at Nazarene Theological Seminary, Kansas City, Missouri, 1957.

world, is that master key that will bring harmony, a harmony so seldom played by the world's symphony. The search for harmony is not a new quest nor an unnatural goal. The quest for hope, as well as the tension between creation and destruction, between life and death, began at the advent of creation. The "not yet" was, and continues to be, the norm and gives the rationale to accept discord, discord that could be tuned but is not.

The search for harmony is not a new quest. Across the spectrum of human creation and life, the picture and the sound of life have not been projected on the screen of experience. Always there was the sense of a "not yet," the promise of hope to be fulfilled. From the Old Testament and pre-Old Testament era, human beings have sought answers to life's pain and the ever-present specter of death. The cries for harmony echoed seemingly to no avail in the concert halls of life . . . until a sound comes from beyond. The creator would send his Son to create a symphony of hope and his Son, as the master conductor, would call for participants to play a new sound, a sound waited for across the centuries.

The call for peace and love that have continued to echo in the halls of life can, and will, be heard if, and when, humanity decides to follow the score written by the author of hope, the master conductor, the risen Christ.

In a world that seems to almost ignore death, the need is for proponents of hope to let the sounds of hope be heard. The sound of hope can and will be heard when individuals, both alone and collectively, begin to make all things new—new in regard to holding life and its value for all in the present and the future. Isn't it amazing, in a tragic sense, that modern technology, with its ever increasing ability to rejuvenate and participate in making a better world, repeats the archaic pattern of destroying in place of creating new aspects of life?

This almost macabre approach to life and death has permeated our modern society by glamorizing war and the rape of the earth. New discords? No, the same failed method of strength, of destruction, while ignoring the real self, the spirit within.

Our universe and those beyond are not creations of a closed mind but reflect visions beyond human imagination. Only when we begin to see and hear participants joining in a symphony of hope can even a minute vision of the magnificence of reality be encountered. Despite the dual proponents of doom regarding the universe, both secular scientists in the field of cosmology and the fundamentalists who resign creation to evil except for the chosen few, the real answer is found in hope. Yes, the revolutionary dynamics of hope projected in this work are the only answer.

Whenever we allow our finite mind to go beyond, as well as beneath, our inner psyche, a new dimension will appear. That new dimension is a revisioning, a renewal of our projection of spirit and the ultimate cause of the new. While the experiences of Viktor Frankl in surviving the death camps was made possible because of his search for meaning, temporal logic and experience tell us that this can be related to the very concept of reality in its more inclusive being. As Frankl notes so clearly and hopefully, "Although we only see our [material, physical] world . . . a still wider world may be there . . . unseen by us . . . "[16] Eschatological reality is that which initiates in our minds another look, another way, a way beyond our finite vision.

To find a valid eschatological sound in this world is to find the true key to hope in both here and beyond time. The concept of our being in process until the end of time is of ultimate importance. For life to be life, there must always be the rebuilding of life's selves, its very essence, not only in the microcosm of life but in the incompleteness of the universe. Process for life and a process for aliveness and purpose is a truism.

As Brian Greene has stated, "Maybe . . . the universe has already drawn out the microscopic fibers of the fabric of the cosmos and unfurled them clear across the sky, and all we need do is learn how to recognize the pattern . . . But for me, there would be nothing more poetic, no outcome more graceful, no unification more complete, than for us to confirm our theories of the ultra-small—our theories about the ultramicroscopic makeup of space, time, and matter—by turning our most powerful telescopes skyward and gazing silently at the stars."[17]

Suddenly we may begin to realize that while we cannot fathom the enormous complexity of the cosmos, perhaps there is a connective fabric that is as close as we are to ourselves. If so, we can cease becoming, as is often thought, astronomically intimidated. We are part of the greater design for eternity, or as I would designate, "progressive permanence." No, we need not fear exploration, for in hope we are part of a new creation. While people are often gripped by the fear of the unknown, waiting to

---

16. Frankl, *The Unconscious God*, 142.

17. Greene, *The Fabric of the Cosmos*, 493.

hear the sound of hope, they can already depend on a hope that they are not lost on a meaningless planet, destined for oblivion in an incomprehensible universe. Only the entrance of a person into this eschatological drama can transform their fears into joy, the joy that hope can be fulfilled by the presence of the risen Christ. Then the promise, the presence of this other, can and will begin a new sound of the symphony of hope, calling everyone to participate. Discords do not need to reign!

A relevant statement regarding the need for action is set forth in William Schweiker's monograph when he says that, "To live the new creation is to dedicate one's life to combat all that unjustly demeans and destroys life out of a profound love of life and in the name of divine goodness. It is even to love the enemy."[18] Too often we fail to see the enemy as a person also in need of the divine person as much as ourselves. A universe is a unity, and we are to be part of this unity.

The discord that we have portrayed in this portion of our writing can only be solved if we really accept the dynamic impact of eschatology. As has been unabashedly noted throughout this study, we do live in a state ever relevant to an eschatological view of reality.

As Schweiker further notes regarding our relationship to time, space, and the universe of which we are a part, "We are not lost in an ocean of meaningless time or awaiting the damnation of the evil. The Christian eschatological witness is that we live within the theater of God's goodness and therefore we are required and empowered to respect and enhance the integrity of life. On this account of new creation, the sciences help us to understand the shape, direction, and limitations of reality and thus fund Christian moral reflection."[19] Yes, there is a thread of universal reality that can and will make sense in a world of discord.

Our essential theme in this work, as we have used the metaphor of music as a vehicle, is that there can and will be harmony if and when we human beings recognize the interrelationship of all creation. We seem to forget or ignore all too quickly the fact that relationships do matter. Perhaps even now as we seek to continue our quest for harmony in the seemingly discordant world, one missing key to the score is that cosmology has often been relegated to just an interesting scientific question not

18. Schweiker, "Time as a Moral Space," 138.
19. Ibid.

really relevant to everyday living. Yet what is more relevant than seeing the possibility of cosmic harmony? We are in this cosmos.

Sometimes as I survey work related to this theme, I am pleasantly surprised to see that even decades ago, the idea that existence is only an event in a meaningless world was being challenged. One of those challengers was a Methodist bishop! As the reader will see, this was no ordinary leader; it was the late Gerald Kennedy. Always deeply courteous, even with those with those with whom he would strongly disagree, Kennedy said, he admired the courage of the secularists who were trying to say some hopeful words in the face of the threat of complete extinction. (This was in the era of the Cold War with its accompanying fear of nuclear weapons.) But their words have a hollow sound, for they are fooling no one but themselves.

Once more we refer to Dr. Einstein's affirmation that matter and energy are interchangeable. Yet in our modern, sophisticated age of so-called thinkers, too many rely on only the material, the part of life that we designate as matter. Whether one is a believer or not in the usual connotation of the word, all human beings live in a world, a cosmos, that is in discord, while seeking harmony.

Anthony Reading, in his work entitled *Hope and Despair*, had a subtitle heading "How Perceptions of the Future Shape Human Behavior." Certainly that is a relevant picture of not only our world of today, but also that of the known and unknown past. Human beings do have a choice about how they see and shape the future.[20] The results are all too evident. While great advances have occurred and continue to expand beyond human imagination, our eschatological view of reality is too often ignored or relegated to an unneeded sound. True hope can only be validated if it has a base beyond the present. The symphony of hope that the world waits to hear has a major key missing, unless the symphony is played in an eschatological score. For hope can only be heard and played in harmony if there is an auditorium to be performed in: the earth in which we live. As Reading has cogently stated, "We are the only species that has a true awareness of time, a sense of having a past, a present, and a future."[21] Thus if we accept this fact, we cannot hear or listen to true sounds of reality unless we deal with the eschatological dynamics of all of life.

20. Reading, 118.
21. Ibid.

In a cosmos with its ever-expanding impact on both our macro-cosmos and micro-cosmos, a developing psychologist such as the late James Loder projects a sound that is held amidst the cacophony of sound of despair. This universe, of which each of us both individually and collectively are a part, is our home, not as a temporary visitor but a vital and eternal member. For those who would negate any assurance of eternal life, an exacting note from Loder must be written into a valid symphony of hope, as he plays a score such as the following.

As Loder notes, there is an ultimate solution to death. Yes, death shocks and depresses us with a seeming finality but only for those in a chronologically locked mindset. Those who have seen and experienced spirited transformation may accept the concept of life after death according to God's promises. Yes, we can be free from the dread of life's ultimate negation.[22] There is an inward longing within this number for eternal intimacy. This, for Loder, is the sense of a presence beyond our finite limits.

To quote Loder here, as he defines what a human being really is: "A lifetime is an unfinished act of God's love; it is intended that we complete that act by returning ourselves to God directly and through others in love. In this recognition we discover that the fundamental data about us are not that we are alive and developing incredible products of an expanding universe, but that we have been created for nothing less than the pure love of God whose universe is our home."[23]

To love in this vast universe, one is often tempted to feel out of tune in this awesome concert hall experience until we recognize our importance as players in this symphony of the universe, complete only by the one who is the creator and conductor of universal harmony.

22. Loder, *The Logic of Spirit*, 340–41.
23. Ibid., 362.

Chapter 8

Sounds of Hope
in "The Unfinished Symphony"

Is ANYTHING REALLY FINISHED? Is anyone ever finished? Only if we accept that life is a process, for in reality, it is impossible to finish any part of creation because matter and its other form, energy, are interchangeable.

And so with hope. In its very definition, it speaks of the "more," the reach beyond . . . the "other way." Thus, as we continue our vision of hope in the metaphor of music, this latter portion of our work once more focuses on Moltmann's expression, "in the end, the beginning." So it is with our section entitled "The Unfinished Symphony." Despite new sounds of hope projected and surveyed, there will always be more. Why? Because if all is achieved, what would one hope for?

To envision a world without hope would be to affirm the emptiness of life, of purpose, of every created entity or being. In essence, creation would be spiraling down into nonexistence. In this work we have dared to enter into areas of the natural sciences, e.g., cosmology, despite not being trained in this vital study. If we look at the cosmos of which all creation is a part, all of our studies must be tuned to its sounds. The sound emanating from theology, psychology, philosophy, and all humanities will be stifled if all of creation is destined for extinction. Thus, all sounds of hope would cease if there is no cosmos to emit these sounds, however beautiful.

The anticipated symphony of hope on which we are focusing will need an auditorium in which to play: that jewel of the cosmos, planet Earth. Oh, yes, it would be helpful to have a few musicians left to play their parts in the auditorium of Earth! To envision hope, the fact of an adequate eschatology is certainly paramount. Unless there is a valid rationale for survival, all of our sounds of hope would be an exercise in futility.

While the incompleteness of this world is very much in evidence, so, too, is our attempt at building a symphony of hope. Just as there is a literal "Unfinished Symphony," so, too, is this study, and by its very incompleteness gives credence to hope, for hope is always both present and future. In other words, there must always be a new horizon, and hope will always call us to "the new."

In contrast to the thinking of Freud and those of his persuasion who saw death and extinction as the end of all creation or life, our theology of hope speaks a resounding "No" to despair. There is more to life than our myopic vision can see. Returning to basic physics, which affirms the interrelationship of energy and matter, the visual and the concrete, are not the whole of reality. Even now the latest studies in psychology are noting the reality of spirit, that there is something beyond the mind-body model. A courageous Freud faced death with stoicism while the darkness closed in. He saw no light at the end of his tunnel nor hope that he needed to hear, as do all human beings. Only empty sounds in a tunnel leading to darkness and despair would meet his senses.

In contrast to this approach, a theology of hope gives us a new tune, a new sound, the sound of caring, loving, creating, and sharing. This, while unfinished, is the real answer to the despair, the loneliness, and the meaninglessness of our society and the individuals who compose it. As we explore the concept of the future, of the really new, it is hope that is the dynamic that sets this in motion. The promise of a new creation is not an idle exercise by theologians of various persuasions, for a basic cosmology and a sensible eschatology, demands this. Human beings are designed to hope, and this hope will be fulfilled.

Now I am deeply aware that in a world of change for the post-modernist, modernists and fundamentalists are irrelevant, but to deny meaning as an imperative in life would be to thrust aside some of the key concepts of such major thinkers as Viktor Frankl and others. As one who has listened to the innumerable sounds of despair, both as a minister and as a counselor, I am ever more aware of the need for people to hear sounds of hope—not only the client, but the therapist as well. The negative sounds, so much in evidence via the mass media, are too often heard in churches as well as secular society. Despairingly enough, those who are to be purveyors of hope too often project a sound of hopelessness. But hopefully this is not the total sound nor picture of life. New horizons are being visited. The hope theologian, Carl Braaten, more than thirty years ago, made a statement that is very much in tune with today's world that is so out of tune. Braaten said, "The Christian gospel is relevant to man because it announces the coming of the future for which man as man hopes, that is, the future of identity-in-fulfillment. The first-fruits of this future identity-in-fulfillment have been born already from the grave. To that extent, there is an element of actualization in eschatology. Only in the resurrection of Christ has the future of life for which men hope been realized on the far side of death. A Christian theology that takes its eschatology seriously has to be a theology formed by the event of Easter."[1]

Yes, there is and can be a new horizon, a hope beyond this finite world. Only a symphony of hope can and will compose a harmony whereby individuals begin to participate by building and living in two worlds. We need to hear sounds of the beyond, a beyond that is close to God's creation. How will we participate and play in this symphony? By playing notes of love, caring, and sharing in a future that is also our "now." In a world living in a state of silence regarding hope and fearing to take a leap of faith, only one can break this silence: the risen Christ, the master conductor, waiting to conduct a new symphony of hope.

A deep pall of gloom has darkened our world, and silence is often the only "sound" heard regarding the future. Nevertheless, there is a future: a future of God. Whenever his creation decides to play in harmony, there will come a new creation—a world designed to play new notes of hopes being fulfilled. As Moltmann has noted, "different forms of despair cannot prevail against the creative power of hope."[2]

Today, as every day, I read the reports of death and despair and hear the discordant sounds of hopelessness, but when I begin to listen to the "still, small voice within," I hear sounds of hope by the composer of hope, the risen Christ. If I listen to the sounds of children and those of older years who see beauty in life, I know that there will be a new symphony of hope—a sound for which the world is almost afraid to listen.

All of us, if we are being honest with ourselves, at times wish we could be in the Land of Beginning Again, as told in various stories of imagination. If we begin to look at the power of hope, the hope coming from its creator, then we can affirm as Moltmann proclaims, "In the end is the beginning!" Yes, reality is in process and is always more than our

1. Braaten and Jenson, *The Futurist Option*, 81–82.
2. Moltmann, *In the End*, 94.

human minds can imagine. To hear the magnificent unfinished symphony played by master musicians, past and present in many great orchestras, is to hear a creation of sound and beauty, and yet we feel there has to be more. As we listen to the discord in this world in which we live, the sound of the unfinished is heard afresh.

However, when we listen to the sound of an unfinished symphony, whether literal or symbolic as noted, the very fact of its being unfinished tells us that there is more planned by the composer. Yes, the God of creation has written a symphony of hope, but in a world of free choice and its many discords, he waits for his creation to participate in a new symphony, a symphony of hope. This symphony of hope, in a very real sense, is composed by those who take seriously the word of the risen Christ, who calls us to participate in life's unfinished symphony.

Yet this call by the master conductor, while being heard, if often responded to by each playing in his or her own key and composition, not that which is composed by the master conductor and author of hope. When all begin to play their assigned parts and key, then and only then, will the sound of hope echo across the valley of despair and the hopelessness of death. We are called by the master conductor to participate but we dare not rewrite the original score!

Only as we begin to play according to the notes of the true score will the reality of hope, its power, its possibility in the face of impossibility, be heard. Until we begin to participate in the symphony of hope, we will find ourselves living with what Tillich designates as "existential anxiety."

The true sound of hope cannot be tuned to this world alone, this moment in time. If one looks at reality in a panoramic view, the concept of eschatology must be explored. For too long this area has been left to the sensationalists, those who build a future on fear and see the Book of Revelation as an invitation to destruction except for the chosen few. But in a world that seems to live in fear of the future, the relevance of eschatology is now very much in evidence. Scholars of the stature of Polkinghorne, Brian Greene, and others, have revisited this ancient yet contemporary scene. Humans, across eons of time, have questioned what is beyond time and what is the future?

The recent conference on eschatology held at the Center for Theological Inquiry at Princeton gave evidence of the relevance of eschatology for a modern age. The unknown was, and continues to be, the focus of every honest theologian and scientist who seeks truth. The birth of hope, while not being new in the sense of its true essence, has brought forth a new interest in theology and science with a need for correlation and co-operation. While a new appreciation for scholars in diverse fields of study is becoming increasingly evident, there is still a gulf that must be crossed.

It must be noted, however, that while the decadent fundamentalists and the old modernists are now elements of the past, the new postmodern age has arrived along with a resurgence of a violent form of evangelicalism. While the postmodernist would tell us there are no absolutes or possibilities for truth, those called evangelical have negated the Prince of Peace, the risen Savior, to accept a stance that "might makes right." Once more we have a collision of ideas resulting in another discord.

Ellen Charry, in an incisive article entitled, "The Valley of Love and Delight," has dealt superbly with this dilemma. The concept that personal freedom is necessary raises the question regarding whether there can be any harmony between different viewpoints at all. In postmodern methodology, anything that hints of order is seen as suspect and alien to Christian belief, i.e., there are no solid realities, and if this is followed, this would apply to science as well.[3] Our answer to such postmodern thought must be that there is a purpose in life and in the cosmos, and that harmony is and will be possible where hope is fulfilled as designed by the master conductor, the risen Christ. We hear sounds of the unfinished symphony as noted in this work, but with the belief that there is and ever will be a purpose, a goal, and something beyond. Hope becomes that which opens to another way.

Our culture demands answers to its call for meaning. The concept of knowing is not an archaic icon of the past. It is still not only possible, but the ultimate element in constructing a theory and psychology of hope that can integrate itself in a cosmology of not only the present, but of the future. For if we can begin to listen to the needs of the world in a state of almost constant disharmony, we will respond by offering to this world the God of hope who calls everyone to participate in his symphony of hope. This symphony of hope is certainly "unfinished," but so is the God of hope, who is ever enlisting more participants to play in his symphony, a symphony of hopes being fulfilled.

In every field of study, the goal is to advance knowledge and to succeed in a particular area. But in a literal symphony, as in our metaphorical

3. Charry, "The Valley of Love and Delight," 462.

symphony of hope, each instrument, each participant must relinquish superiority in their areas of expertise in order to build a symphonic sound. As we survey the various areas of study, both in the humanities and those in the natural sciences, the key is to accept and complement each others' sounds to build a unified sound.

Happily there is a greater response from the other fields of study as scholars are seeing and hearing valid sounds from multiple sources. No longer do those in the empirical fields of science diminish the sounds in the fields of humanities, including that oft forgotten area of theology. Our need is to see beyond our own areas and initiate a correlation between multiple areas of study. Yes, there can and will be a symphony of hope—if only an unfinished symphony.

We do live in an unfinished world. It is also a world of contradiction, even in the realm of nature, however beautiful it may appear. Natural disasters of incomparable proportions appear with no guarantee that they can or will be controlled. Untold suffering and a feeling of loneliness even in a crowd seems to occur despite the acceptance of a caring God and his Son, the risen Christ. Yes, discords are so very real and a minor key of life visibly seems to dominate.

The label "a Christian America" becomes, in essence, only a name, a description of an imaginary time in history that never was, but because there never was a Christian America does not negate the fact that the risen Christ is unheard. In reality it is only because of the Christ, his gift of hope and healing, that the symphony of hope will be heard. Despite all of the discords of life, its confusion and misdirection, when the master conductor takes control, the new and eternal sound of hope will fill the empty halls of life. Suddenly, there will be a sense of presence, the presence of one who can and will bring harmony and healing to a world so out of tune.

There is darkness and sounds of hate and death in this world. But one should ever be reminded of the old but relevant adage, "All the darkness of the world cannot put out a single candle." We can complete this saying, offering the world the candle of hope.

In the unfinished symphony, there was, and must ever be, a sense of what could or must be. And the God of hope who once entered the auditorium of planet Earth will prevail, though still self-limiting. God is still the ultimate conductor, the master composer, for whom the audience awaits.

Our creator God has given us the Christ of hope, the risen Christ, to be the finger of God pointing into our world, as Pannenberg once noted.[4] Is this possible in a world so filled with fear of the unknown, with almost constant sounds of terror that drown out sounds that tell of hope? Yes, for the same sounds of despair that came from the hammer blows as the Christ of hope was being crucified are now sounds of the past, and because of the risen Christ, who experienced these sounds, there is a new sound of life and love. Despite the sounds that seemed muffled by hate, a new harmony emerged above the sounds that were so terribly off-key.

How and why? Because one came from beyond, being a personification of hope incarnate. The sounds of hate and hopelessness, once so very loud and clear, were broken by one who said, "I am alive forevermore." He had heard the sound of life and hope from beyond. His God would raise from the darkness of despair and death, and now a new harmony would be played. As the light of Easter morning would break forth, the real score of hope would be opened, and though unfinished, the symphony of hope would begin. We who at best are only elementary participants in the symphony of hope are called to share the music, and there are no auditions . . . only additions for all humanity.

Hope in all its dynamics and very essence is always open and tells us that there is another way. The unfinished symphony continues to play, waiting for its completion in the eschaton. The questions will now arise: where and when will the symphony be completed, and by whom? The answer can only be given as we listen to contemporary sounds of progress, progress toward completing the unfinished symphony. The unfinished symphony is beautiful in its own right, but it is nevertheless waiting for someone somewhere to complete its masterful composition. And we are to be co-composers!

A world so very incomplete and yet so complete in its pain and loneliness and meaninglessness is seeking wholeness amidst its brokenness. A symphony of hope is waiting to be completed, but it is ever in need for its language to be translated for all to hear its true sound, the sound of hope.

The statement that music is the universal language is true, especially as we extend and explore via the metaphor of music relating to the sound of hope in human expression. In a world so filled with languages and yet so empty of relationship, the sound of hope is yet uncommunicated

---

4. Pannenberg, *Jesus, God and Man.*

among its inhabitants. While new ways of communication are constantly being designed and made available, hollow sounds of loneliness echo in the homes and workplaces of all humanity. Messages are sent and received with ever increasing speed and efficiency, but the language of love, the language of the creator, is heard infrequently.

Hope, while based upon both subjective and empirical facts, is having its reality written in exciting and refreshing new ways. In the not-too-distant past, humankind has crossed a bridge into a momentous new era. As Dr. Francis Collins so incisively noted, "an announcement beamed around the world, highlighted in virtually all major newspapers, the first draft of the human genome, our own instruction book, has been assembled."[5]

And as would be expected, interpreters from both spectrums of thought, both the right and the left, were once more in conflict. The fundamentalist mindset and its adherents affirmed that science, that "scourge of religion," was tampering with God's creative power, and across the spectrum of thought, the postmodern and secular thinkers now had proof that God was never a necessity to begin with. Thus, only human beings were in complete control, not only of life but, in essence, its very creation.

Could it be that, as Freud and others decades ago proclaimed, what and whom we call God is our own creation? But if we explore the true dynamics of hope and belief in God, the fact remains that hope is not based only on human imagination, but on empirical reality—a reality that has written and created and continues to write and create ever new achievements. All achievements must first begin with hope, the hope that creation will be achieved. For while there remains an unfinished symphony, explorations into the code of life verify that the mystery of life is being shown on the screen of reality.

The affirmation that music is the universal language becomes ever more relevant as we listen to the new sounds of hope being written in the "language of God," as Dr. Collins refers to the discovery of our human genetic code. Yes, amidst the discord so often noted and heard in everyday life, these new sounds of hope are being written not only in the stars of our seemingly incomprehensible universe, but in the silent language of love. For as we see and hear the language of the God of all creation, as

5. Collins, *The Language of God*, 1.

God writes the code of life, each of us may hear the sound of hope from beyond.

This beyond may not be only in the distant and incomprehensible vastness of the universe but in the inner code of us human beings, that unique instrument designed by God to write and play in the symphony of hope. In the groundbreaking work of Francis Collins, one may be able to hear a fresh note of hope that becomes another "key" to the discord of life. The DNA, that which excites those who seek the answers to life's impossibilities, may be that missing note in life's unfinished symphony. We are individuals with our uniqueness but with potential that even now has only been released so minutely. Even as we, in our finitude, stand in awe at the awesomeness of the cosmos, we can affirm that the God who initiated this creation has deposited in our very being that which is the real igniting spark of life, the element of hope.

For when we look at hope as that which is the dynamic of all creation, we may see the symbolic correlation of the DNA as that key and sound that will ever stimulate life into perpetual progress, to a destiny with unimaginable joy: the joy of life unending, ever beginning.

Chapter 9

Sounds of Hope in Progress

THERE IS THE UNFINISHED symphony . . . and because it is unfinished, our challenge is to begin to finish that which is incomplete. Yet because it is incomplete, the fact remains that, in hope, completion will be ever in progress. In a world incomplete with its multiple wounds, its very being seemingly permeated with hopelessness, each participant in a symphony of hope must explore new ways to bring harmony. Yes, harmony, when the raucous sounds of discord have overpowered sounds of joy, peace, love . . . and, to a degree, even hope itself! But hope is not to be denied. By its very definition, it points to an ever new sound. Though it may seem unfinished, and almost silent, hope does break through, and the "unfinished symphony" is in process of being completed.

In the writing of Jürgen Moltmann, the future is projected as a completion, a healing not only of society but of each individual. In the power of God, all of earth's incompletions, its ugly wounds, and death itself will be transformed, and the new sound of joy, of healing and health, will be played by our symphony of hope. In the words of Moltmann, "God the Creator remains faithful to his creation in its redemption too, and 'does not forsake the work of his hands'. He doesn't give anything up for lost and destroys nothing he has made. That is why in the Bible the redemption is called the 'new creation', and this embraces 'everything'. (Rev. 21:5) . . . By this I mean: when our temporal life is transformed into eternal livingness, that life doesn't disappear; it will be 'transfigured'. It will be accepted, put right, reconciled, sanctified, and glorified . . . and for the first time, [we will] come properly and fully to ourselves."[1]

To read the exciting works of Moltmann is to see one who accepts the fact that there is more to life than the present, and there is the hope,

---

1. Moltmann, *In the End*, 161–62.

a sure hope, that in our words the symphony will be played in its fullness. The concrete need to destroy illness and despair is as yet unfinished. There is an ever new horizon awaiting us.

It is concerning these concrete needs that the sound of good news and a future filled with hope is being heard. The life drama, once seemingly closed to hope, with hope being only an idle fantasy or escape from reality, is now opening. The literal power of hope is being felt and coming from those in diverse yet interconnected areas of psychology, theology, philosophy, and science, including cosmology.

In our world of today, with its collision of values and the need for collaboration between society and the individuals that comprise it, the question remains, who and where is that entity called "the person"? The unfinished symphony can only be completed when all participants will converge in trying to tune themselves to the composition written and directed by the master composer, the risen Lord.

But when we envision the hope of all, the greatest achievements in the various areas of study becoming focused on a new symphony of hope, we must once more return to cosmology. The authors of the book *The End of the World and the Ends of God* accepted this challenge. Here scholars in both the humanities and the natural sciences wrestle with the dynamics of cosmology, an area too often ignored by the radicals of both left and right. Teilhard de Chardin's concept of a teleology as the omega point has given us at least a glimmer of hope in seeing how it "all comes together." If we can see a purpose, a goal, a focal point, then and only then, can we hear a true sound of hope, a symphony played by participants following the conductor and his composition. In the works of such individuals as the late Norman Cousins and the contemporary works of Bernie Seigel, Carl Simonton, and others, the unity of life is set forth with a focus on wholeness—in other words, harmony. For thinkers in this category, humans are more than a collocation of atoms and molecules. There is an inner "something" we are daring to call spirit. As we listen to the new sounds of hope echoing from seeing humans and their universe as being part of each other, harmony would seem to be heard. Our need is to listen to the sound from beyond, from "another land," as Ben Campbell Johnson notes.[2]

---

2. Johnson, *Living Before God*, 21.

The human document, the living human document, must choose to initiate harmony, the harmony that has been negated in the past and is now being played by players in many fields, which becomes clear when we take a synoptical view of human beings. It is this writer's firm conviction that we are programmed for harmony, a harmony designed by our creator, the master conductor and composer.

To be alive is to be in progress, and to be open to the new is not to ignore the past. Therefore we must always measure our progress by its value, its contribution to the symphony of hope. Decades ago the late Paul Tillich used the phrase "the eternal now," and how relevant that statement is in this age of change. It is a tragic fact that a world so out of tune listens to a futureless, non-eschatalogical mode of thinking that borders on nihilism. But we do have a choice. We do not have to wander in the dark night of despair, for even in the night of despair, we can listen for a song. Today it is very exciting to hear these new sounds of hope played to an audience anxious to attend, to see beyond the visual, the concrete, and to begin to hear true sounds of hope—hope in process of being fulfilled. Today scientists of incomparable status are becoming some of the most holistic instrumentalists in the symphony of hope. Harmony is now being heard and transposed.

For while it is still popular to be filled with skepticism negating an experience more than the "now," the real thinkers, the Einsteins, the Polkinghornes, the Menningers, and the Jungs are only a minute portion of the ever increasing number of the intelligentsia who see and hear beyond the present. As Hans Weder notes, "Hope, the practical and concrete approach to eschatology, has not fallen out of the blue; it rather is nourished by earthly experience."[3] Yes, the concept of hope is not only "beyond," but is very earthly!

In fact, that is what the incarnation of our Lord was, a very earthly experience, an experience of the God beyond in the here and now. To look at the present and then to the future is an ever shortening opportunity unless there is more hope. It is hope that is the key to open up our tomorrows.

The world in which we live is, and remains, a quandary. As we look with our finite vision at this incomplete universe here and beyond, a sense of astronomical intimidation may occur once again. Nevertheless,

---

3. Weder, "Hope and Creation," in *The End of the World and the Ends of God*, 184.

because of that ever present element of hope, the future is open—open to envision more of reality.

As Trinh Xuan Thuan has noted, the secret melody of the universe "will remain forever inaccessible" and yet, Thuan states, we must never abandon the search; the universe still beckons for us to explore its very inaccessibility.[4] Fragments of knowledge that we can grasp give us a hint. Our need as human beings will always be to explore the understanding even though the answer is one of impossible proportions.

Nevertheless, because of its very impossibility for us to comprehend, new possibilities will continue. Because of hope, that incomprehensible element that draws us toward the new future, we created entities, finite though we are, may become co-creators of the new! An awesome concept, but so very possible. When we look at the universe as "uni-verse," we are all united. Despite the skeptics and radical interpretations of that misunderstood Book of Revelation, the truth remains that because of the risen Christ, all will become new. For that reality, we await and yet move in anticipation of its fulfillment. But the question must then be asked, fulfilled for what and to what degree? For the cosmologist Thuan, we need to hear the music of the stars, and even though the cosmos is so vast, it is by no means silent; it is like a far-off symphony tantalizing us with a fragment of a symphony, but the melody linking bits and pieces is missing. The task of science is to unveil the secret of this hidden melody so that we can listen to its composition in all its glory.[5]

Despite having only fragments of knowledge, it is a fragment that may stimulate us to follow the star of hope as we minute, yet favored, creations of our creator engage in writing a symphony of hope. As Polkinghorne has noted in his recent work, *Science and Providence: God's Interaction with the World*, the infinite God is a source of inexhaustible hope both in the process of the world and beyond it. This hope is based on the God who can interact with the world in many ways, more particularly than just a general willing of its existence. This hope is a coherent possibility within the framework provided by the scientific understanding of the cosmic process.[6]

---

4. Thuan, *The Secret Melody*, 274.

5. Ibid.

6. Polkinghorne, *Science and Providence*, 48.

In this work, our focus has been that of projecting a new vision of the validity of hope, not based on wishful thinking, but on a hope congruent with reality. This new sound of hope must be played not by isolated soloists, however proficient, but by all participants in multiple areas of expertise. The new sound of hope and the symphony must be performed by theologians, psychologists, natural scientists, and last but not least, by cosmologists. If we hope to build a lasting symphony of hope, its sound will come not only from a purely empirical source but from one that draws its spirit from the hope generated by the risen Christ.

The sound of hope has been heard and will be heard above the cacophony of hopelessness and despair. We await in hope this total performance when all will be in harmony. No, there are not enough participants in the symphony of hope, but we must remember that the master conductor, who has already written the new score, the ultimate symphonic creation, is still with us. Even now he is seeking for all to participate. Yes, the future of God has arrived, though yet in progress. The God of the future is in reality never one to close off applications for new participants. In God's view, as noted throughout this work, the end is ever a new beginning, and creation is in process.

The exciting truth is that, with all of our incompleteness, we have a definitive relationship with the universe and the God who created it. Perhaps few, if any, contemporary writers have set forth this truth more beautifully than the theologian-scientist Alister McGrath as he states, "The same God who created the universe also created us. There is thus a created resonance between ourselves and the universe. We are enabled to hear the music of its creator and discern the hand of the creator within its beauty. It is part of the purpose of the creator that we should hear the music of the cosmos, and, through loving its harmonies, come to love their composer."[7] Let the concert begin!

7. McGrath, *Glimpsing the Face of God*, 48.

Postlude

WE HAVE HEARD THE prelude. We have read and listened to the dynamics of hope, at least in part. Each chapter has sounded its specific notes of an expression of hope. Now it is time to leave the concert hall as we listen to the postlude. If we listen, really listen, we will hear the theme of hope being sounded again and again even as we rejoin the noisiness of the world outside the doors of the concert hall.

Because we have heard at least in part, we will be aware of a new sound, a sound of hope from the beyond, coming to the "now" of our lives. This new sound of hope cannot be stifled or forgotten. To listen to this sound and to respond to its message is to negate the sounds of despair and hopelessness. These latter sounds will no longer be heard as we replace them with the sounds of love and hope in action. An oft-wounded creation distorted by hate and despair will hear the new sounds of hope, not in desolation, but in recreation in the life of hope eternal.

Bibliography

Berkhof, Hendrikus. *Well-Founded Hope*. Richmond, VA: John Knox, 1969.

Braaten, Carl E. *Eschatology and Ethics: Essays on the Theology and Ethics of the Kingdom of God*. Minneapolis: Augsburg, 1974.

———. *Mother Church: Ecclesiology and Ecumenism*. Minneapolis: Fortress, 1998.

Braaten, Carl E., and Robert Jenson. *The Futurist Option*. New York: Newman, 1970.

Burton, Arthur. *Interpersonal Psychotherapy*. Englewood Cliffs, NJ: Prentice-Hall, 1972.

Capps, Donald. *Agents of Hope: A Pastoral Psychology*. Minneapolis: Fortress, 1995.

Charry, Ellen. "The Valley of Love and Delight." *Theology Today* 62/4 (January 2006): 459–64.

Clinebell, Howard. "Religion Can Make You Sick or Keep You Well." (Unpublished manuscript, December 2004).

Collins, Francis S. *The Language of God: A Scientist Presents Evidence for Belief*. New York: Free Press, 2006.

Cousins, Norman. *Anatomy of an Illness as Perceived by the Patient: Reflections on Healing and Regeneration*. New York: Bantam, 1981.

———. *Head First: The Biology of Hope*. New York: Penguin, 1989.

Cox, Richard H. *The Sacrament of Psychology: Psychology and Religion in the Postmodern American*. Sanford, FL: Insync, 2002.

Greene, Brian. *The Fabric of the Cosmos: Space, Time, and the Texture of Reality*. New York: Vintage, 2004.

Groopman, Jerome. *The Anatomy of Hope: How People Prevail in the Face of Illness*. New York: Random House, 2004.

Emmons, Robert A. *The Psychology of Ultimate Concerns: Motivation and Spirituality in Personality*. New York: Guilford, 1995.

Farley, W. Edward. "Can Preaching Be Taught?" *Theology Today* 62/2 (July 2005): 171–80.

Frankl, Viktor E. *The Unconscious God:Psychotherapy and Theology*. New York: Simon and Schuster, 1975.

———. *The Unheard Cry for Meaning: Psychotherapy and Humanism*. New York: Simon and Schuster, 1978.

Janacek, Robert. "A Theology and Psychology of Hope in Clergy." D. Min. thesis, Boston University, 1991.

Johnson, Ben Campbell. *Living Before God: Deepening Our Sense of the Divine Presence*. Grand Rapids: Eerdmans, 2000.

Johnson, Paul E. *Psychology of Religion*. New York: Abingdon-Cokesbury, 1945.

Jones, James W. "Religion, Health, and the Psychology of Religion: How the Research on Religion and Health Helps Us Understand Religion." *Journal of Religion and Health* 43/4 (Winter 2004): 317–28.

Jones, Scott. "In Memory of H. Shulte" in *Princeton Theological Review* 6: 32–34.

Bibliography

Juel, Donald. "Christian Hope and the Denial of Death." In *The End of the World and the Ends of God: Science and Theology on Eschatology*, edited by John Polkinghorne and Michael Welker. Harrisburg, PA: Trinity, 2000.

Lee, Sang Uk. "Constructing an Aesthetic Weltanschauung: Freud, James, and Ricoeur." *Journal of Religion and Health* 43/4 (Winter 2004): 273–290.

Loder, James E. *The Logic of Spirit: Human Development in Theological Perspective*. San Francisco: Jossey-Bass, 1998.

———. *The Transforming Moment*. New York: Harper and Row, 1981.

Marty, Martin E. "Let Us Now Praise: Langdon Brown Gilkey, 1919–2004." *Theology Today* 62/2 (April 2005): 92–96.

McGrath, Alister E. *A Brief History of Heaven*. Walden, MA: Blackwell, 2003.

———. *Glimpsing the Face of God: The Search for Meaning in the Universe*. Grand Rapids: Eerdmans, 2002.

———. *The Unknown God: Searching for Spiritual Fulfilment*. Grand Rapids: Eerdmans, 1999.

Metzger, Bruce. *Breaking the Code:Understanding the Book of Revelation*. Nashville: Abingdon, 1993.

Moltmann, Jürgen. *In the End—the Beginning: The Life of Hope*. Translated by Margaret Kohl. Minneapolis: Fortress, 2004.

Moltmann, Jürgen, and Elisabeth Moltmann-Wendel. *Passion for God: Theology in Two Voices*. Louisville: Westminster John Knox, 2003.

Nichols, J. Randall. *The Restoring Word*. San Francisco: Harper & Sons, 1987.

Pannenberg, Wolfhart. *Jesus, God and Man*. Translated by Lewis L. Wilkens and Duane A. Priebe. Philadelphia: Westminster, 1968.

———. *Metaphysics and the Idea of God*. Translated by Philip Clayton. Grand Rapids: Eerdmans, 1990.

———, ed. *Revelation as History*. Translated by David Granskou. New York: Macmillan, 1968.

———. *What is Man? Contemporary Anthropology in Theological Perspective*. Translated by Duane A. Priebe. Philadelphia: Fortress, 1970.

Polkinghorne, John C. Review of *In the Beginning . . . Creativity* by Gordon Kaufman. *Theology Today* 62/2 (July 2005): 264–6.

———. *Science and Providence: God's Interaction with the World*. Philadelphia: Templeton Foundation, 1989.

Polkinghorne, John, and Michael Welker, eds. *The End of the World and the Ends of God: Science and Theology on Eschatology*. Harrisburg, PA: Trinity, 2000.

Powery, Luke A. "Death Threat: 1 Corinthians 11:17–34a." *The Princeton Seminary Bulletin* 28/3 (2007): 244–50.

Reading, Anthony. *Hope and Despair: How Perceptions of the Future Shape Human Behavior*. Baltimore: The Johns Hopkins University Press, 2004.

Schuller, Robert H. *Don't Throw Away Tomorrow: Living God's Dream for Your Life*. San Francisco: Harper, 2005.

Schweiker, William. "Time as a Moral Space: Moral Cosmologies, Creation, and Last Judgment." In *The End of the World and the Ends of God: Science and Theology on Eschatology*, edited by John Polkinghorne and Michael Welker. Harrisburg, PA: Trinity, 2000.

Siegel, Bernie. *Love, Medicine, and Miracles: Lessons Learned about Self-Healing from a Surgeon's Experience with Exceptional Patients*. New York: HarperCollins, 1988.

———. *Peace, Love and Healing: Bodymind Communication and the Path to Self-Healing: An Exploration.* New York: HarperCollins, 1990.

Strunk, Orlo, Jr. "Religion as Deviant Reality: The Psychology Theory Dilemma." *National Guild of Catholic Psychiatrists* 29 (1983): 29–35.

———. "The Role of Visioning in the Pastoral Counseling Movement." *Pastoral Psychology* 31 (Fall 1982): 7–18.

———. "The World View Factor in Psychotherapy." *Journal of Religion and Health* 18/3 (July 1979): 192–6.

Tillich, Paul. *The New Being.* New York: Scribner, 1955.

———. *The Shaking of the Foundations.* New York: Scribner, 1948.

Thielicke, Helmut. *Living with Death.* Translated by Geoffrey Bromiley. Grand Rapids: Eerdmans, 1987.

Thuan, Trinh Xuan. *The Secret Melody: And Man Created the Universe.* Philadelphia: Templeton, 2005.

Tutu, Desmond. *God Has a Dream: A Vision of Hope for Our Time.* New York: Image, 2004.

Weder, Hans. "Metaphor and Reality." In *The End of the World and the Ends of God: Science and Theology on Eschatology,* edited by John Polkinghorne and Michael Welker, 291–7. Harrisburg, PA: Trinity, 2000.

Yaqob, Olga. "The Face of God in Suffering: Iraq." *Theology Today* 62/1 (April 2005): 9–17.

www.ingramcontent.com/pod-product-compliance
Lightning Source LLC
Chambersburg PA
CBHW060429090426
42734CB00011B/2504